TEN SIMPLE SAILING MODELS

Children from 6 to 86 will be fascinated

TEN
SIMPLE SAILING MODELS

Frank Wilson

Nexus Special Interests

Nexus Special Interests Ltd.
Nexus House
Azalea Drive
Swanley
Kent BR8 8HU

First published by Nexus Special Interests Ltd., 1999

All illustrations and diagrams appearing in this book have been originated by the author except where otherwise indicated.

ISBN 1-85486-185-9

Typeset by Kate Williams, Abergavenny
Printed and bound in Great Britain by Bookcraft (Bath) Ltd.

Dedication

This book is dedicated to the many friends I have made in over fifty years of boat modelling. Also to my wife, Barbara, who has had to put up with boats everywhere as well as a boat-mad husband for 47 years.

Contents

Foreword

Daniel, my grandson, aged five, carefully studied the large model clipper I was just finishing. "I bet you had a bit of trouble making *that*" he said. We all had to laugh, of course, but, as it happens, he was quite wrong. The clipper had taken me a couple of hundred hours, I suppose, but I wouldn't call it trouble. A very pleasant way to spend a couple of hours quite regularly maybe, but trouble, no.

My great grandfather, who had been to sea in windjammers, carved me a model ship when I was only five or six and I've been fascinated by ships and the sea ever since. Over the past fifty years or so I have made dozens of models. Some were quite good and won trophies. Even so, when I visit the *Model Engineer's Exhibition* (now the *International Model Show*) in London I usually conclude that I ought to give up making model boats and take up knitting or basketwork! Many of the models there are quite out of my league. However, my doubts never last long and I am soon back to whittling away.

I particularly enjoy making quite simple models to my own design and then testing them to 'see how they go'. This collection of designs includes ten of the better ones. Some designs are old, some quite recent, but they all have one thing in common – they are all quite simple to make.

Much is written these days regarding ways to relieve stress. There is no better way, in my opinion, than to spend a couple of hours, here and there, quietly making something on the kitchen table and what better than a sailing boat? They are clean, silent in use, and environmentally acceptable. Also, you will certainly have a great deal of pleasure sailing those you choose to make. Hopefully, you will meet nice some very nice people, and children, while you are by the water, at school or wherever – I often do.

Introduction

This book is intended to introduce adults and children of school age to the fascinating hobby of making model ships and boats.

There is plenty of evidence to indicate a strong revival in the wish of many people to do something constructive with their leisure time. I recently retired from the Education Service and am now employed part-time in Adult and Further Education. Our practical classes are becoming ever more popular, I believe for the reasons already stated.

The ten designs

Simple 9in. sailboard (first published in* Model Boats, *April 1975)
This little balsa boat can be made by children with adult supervision. It sails (or races) downwind.

A 22in. windsurfer (first published in* Model Boats, *December 1977)
This can also be made by children with adult supervision. Of very simple balsa construction it carries lead ballast and gives a good sailing performance.

Mini tea clipper (first published in* Model Boats, *February 1979)
This model can be made by children aged 13 years or upwards with adult help. I have personally run two project classes with Year 10 students (14/15 year-olds) and had good results. The construction is softwood, balsa, dowel etc. It has a detachable keel so the model can be both displayed and sailed.

Seacat – *a 24in. (610mm) easy-build catamaran (first published in* Model Boats, *April 1984)*
This design has proved popular as a school project for pupils aged 12 years and up. It is a very simple design in softwood which gives a good performance.

A 'J' class sloop (recent design, previously unpublished)
This simple balsa sailing model with a fixed keel and no rudder has been designed with the beginner in mind. A good performer.

Swordfish – *a ketch (recent design, previously unpublished)*
This design is a direct descendant of the mini tea clipper. The hull is almost identical but the rigging is altered to fore and aft. A good performer for its size and suitable for more advanced students, it has a detachable keel.

Sidewinder – *a 30in. outrigger canoe (recent design, previously unpublished)*
This is a simple design in softwood and balsa and very suitable for a school project. It gives a surprising performance with plenty of scope for experimental variations.

Spice Girl – *a 24in. trimaran (recent design, previously unpublished)*
A high-performance boat made almost completely in balsa. This is possibly the most difficult model to make in this collection but only because there are three hulls to make, however they are quite simple to construct. This is a real flyer.

An 18in. scow (recent design, previously unpublished)
This is a very simple 'skimming dish' type in balsa. Although an unconventional model it sails very well.

Nautilus – *an 8in. galleon (recent design, previously unpublished)*
Strictly for fun, this little ship can be made by anyone (children may need some help though). With a detachable keel it can be sailed or displayed. It is not, however, a flyer.

Measurement

I feel I should apologise to the world in general for the parlous state of our measurement system(s) here in the United Kingdom. Being fairly long in the tooth myself I fully understand feet, inches, eighths, sixteenths, etc. However, having worked in a school for the past ten years, I have had to get to grips with the metric system too, but I realise many older people never have. Schools only teach the metric system to our children and so they don't really understand feet and inches.

As a further complication, school technology departments use millimetres whereas science departments use centimetres as well. This country generally hasn't come round to thinking in kilometres yet, but I expect it will come. I believe in the USA they are only just beginning to use metric at all.

As I earnestly hope this book will be enjoyed by young and old, not only here in Great Britain but also in Europe, the United States and everywhere else as well, I hope you will see my difficulty. Having said all that, I find the metric system much easier to use for model making and I hope you will too. It's a mess all right, but none of it is my fault – honestly!

Materials and methods

Balsa wood

Many 'serious' modellers regard balsa as unsuitable because it is easily damaged, however I do not agree. Provided balsa is properly painted it will last indefinitely and is perfectly suitable for the small- to medium-sized sailing models in this book.

Balsa cement is obviously the best glue to use. It is quick and clean to use, and absolutely waterproof. PVA woodworking adhesive can also be used, but takes much longer to set.

A good, tough surface finish is obtained by giving a balsa model three coats of clear polyurethane varnish rubbed over lightly with very fine glasspaper between each coat. Decks can be left without further treatment and the honey colour of balsa is quite attractive. For the rest of the hull, one coat of undercoat and one of gloss completes the job. Provided the hull is not trodden on or otherwise abused, it will last for ever.

Plywood

Small panels can be obtained almost everywhere. The thickness normally required in this book is 4mm or 5mm. Waterproof plywood is not really necessary so long as it is properly painted and not left afloat for days at a time.

For decks it is possible to use very thin marine ply (1mm or 2mm) if you can get it, but it isn't specified on any of these designs.

Dowel for masts and spars

All the masts and spars in this book are from birch or ramin dowel, 6mm, 5mm, 4mm, 3mm thick, widely available. Bamboo kebab sticks are very useful too (available from most supermarkets). Bamboo is incredibly strong and can be split down into fine diameters, but it can be difficult to drill fine holes in it.

Masts should be tapered at the top end and the spars at both ends. This can be done with scrapers and sandpaper, twisting all the time.

For adults (only) a quicker method is to fix one end of the dowel in a portable drill chuck, fold a piece of coarse glasspaper over it held in a gloved hand and switch on. Running the glasspaper along and back on the top half will soon produce a smooth taper. You do need a glove because the glasspaper gets quite hot – you have been warned!

Drilling small holes in masts etc.

A small cordless drill is best, of course, but there are alternatives. Buy a set of watchmaker's screwdrivers. They are quite cheap and the smallest ones make excellent little drills. Just press and keep twisting. A pin vice (a small hand-held chuck) also does the business.

Screweyes for rigging

Small brass screweyes are widely used in making model boats, but only if you can buy them. I am fortunate to have a good ironmongers' shop locally that stocks them. If you manage to find a stockist buy as many as you can afford. The best size has an eye about 2mm or 3mm.

Apart from ironmongers' and model shops, other possible sources of supply are art and craft shops, or picture framers.

Alternatives can be used such as split pins, staples or fine wire twisted into an eye and firmly glued in. Remember such eyes will not hold in balsa – there has to be a strip of 'proper' wood under the balsa.

Thread

Black or brown carpet thread can usually be purchased from shoe repair shops. It is usually bought wound onto a flat card and for rigging on model boats it cannot be beaten. 'Button' thread is useful for lacing sails to masts and binding things to other things. It is much thicker than cotton and is sold on reels.

Sails

I used to find making sails was the most difficult thing to do when making model boats. I had to find someone I could wheedle, flatter or bribe to machine fine fabric into sails. Now, for small

MAKING SAILS

1. TAPE PLASTIC OR GREASEPROOF PAPER TO CUTTING BOARD.

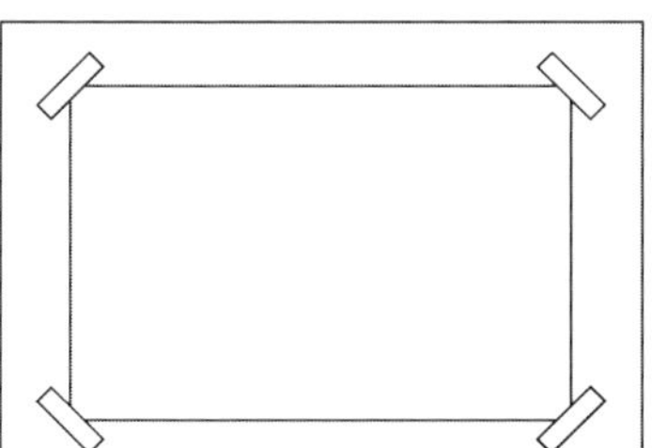

2. STICK MASKING TAPE STRAIGHT ACROSS AND PRESS DOWN FLAT.

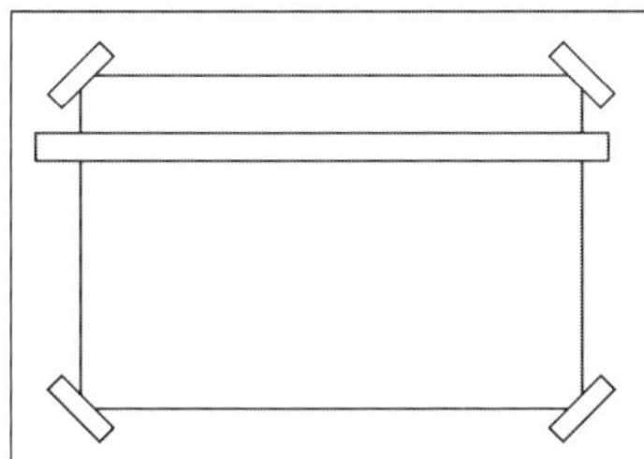

3. MARK A LINE WITH PENCIL TO SHOW EDGE OF SAIL.

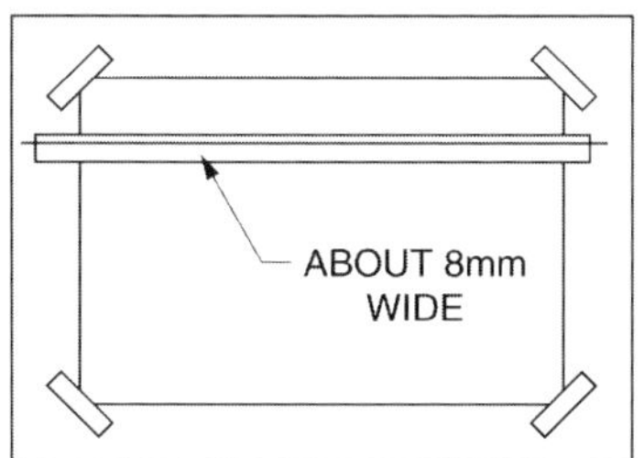

4. CUT OUT SAIL USING CARD PATTERN ALL ROUND

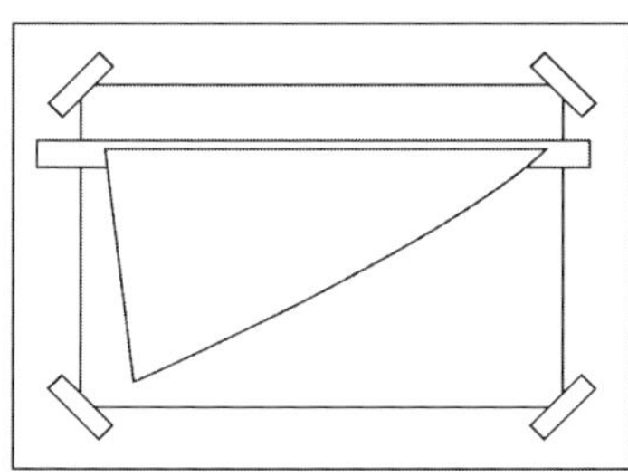

5. CUT OFF WASTE AND REINFORCE CORNERS WITH MASKING TAPE.

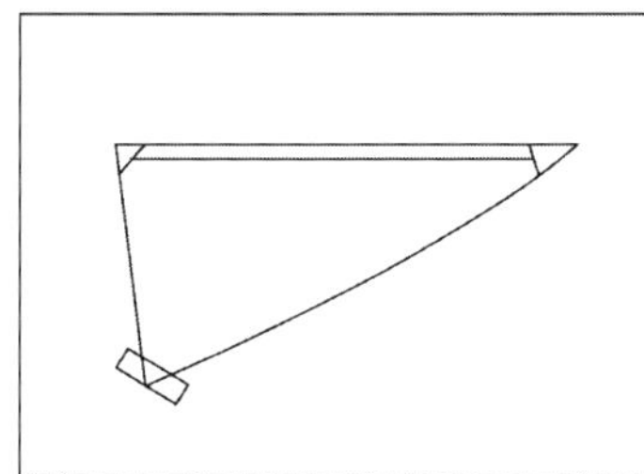

6. PUNCH HOLES AT 30mm - 50mm INTERVALS ALONG LUFF AND AT CLEW.

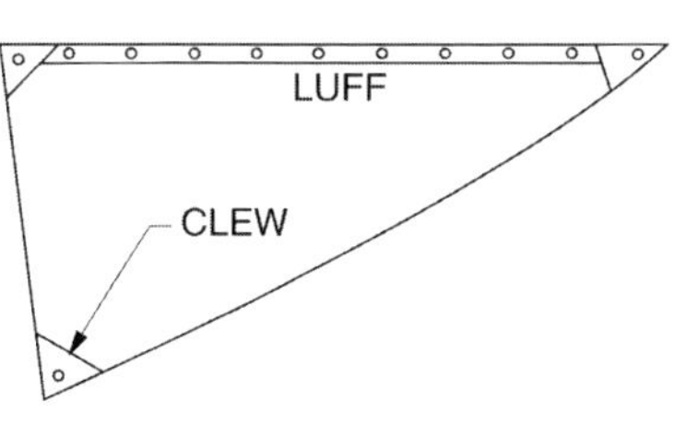

BOOM FITTING TO MAST

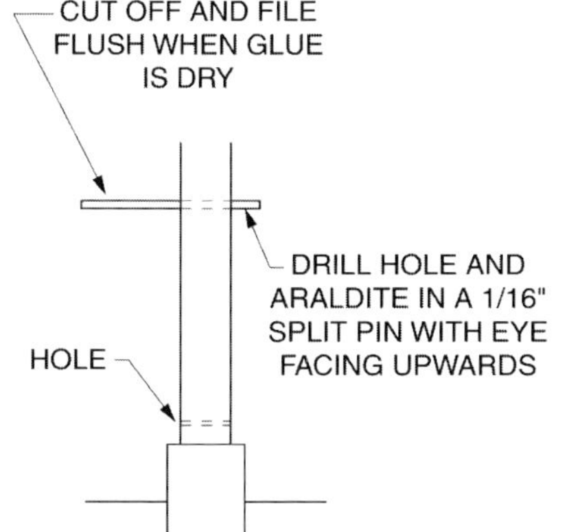

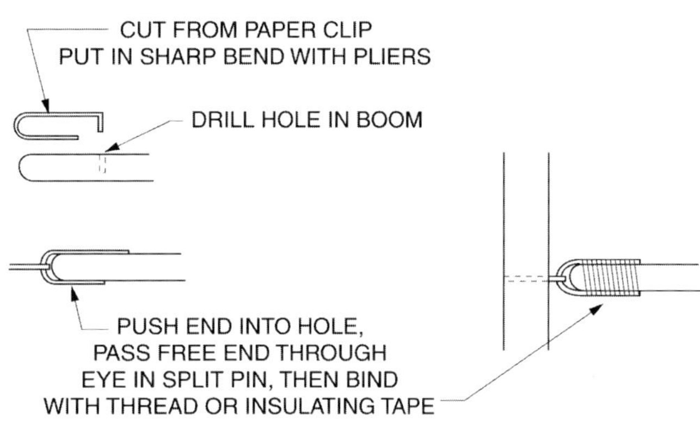

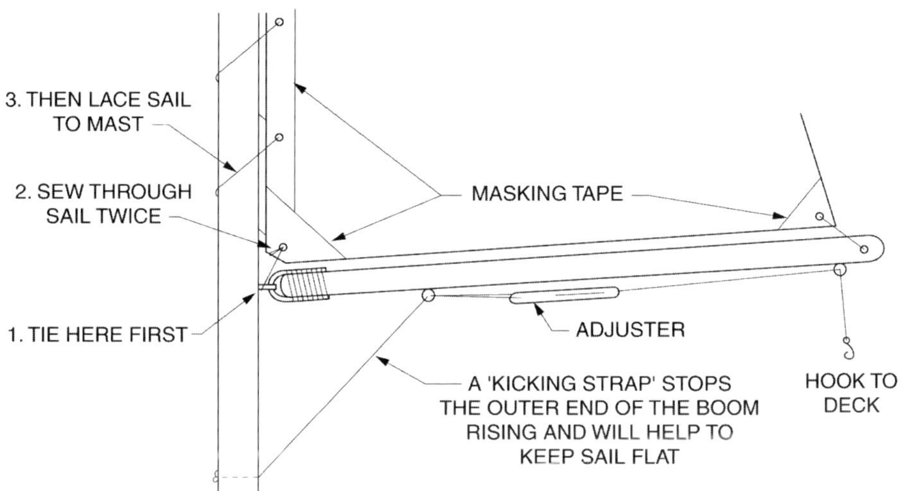

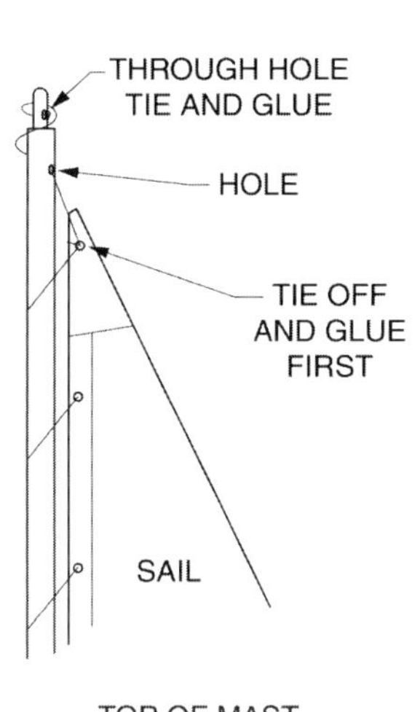

TYPICAL JIB AND FITTINGS

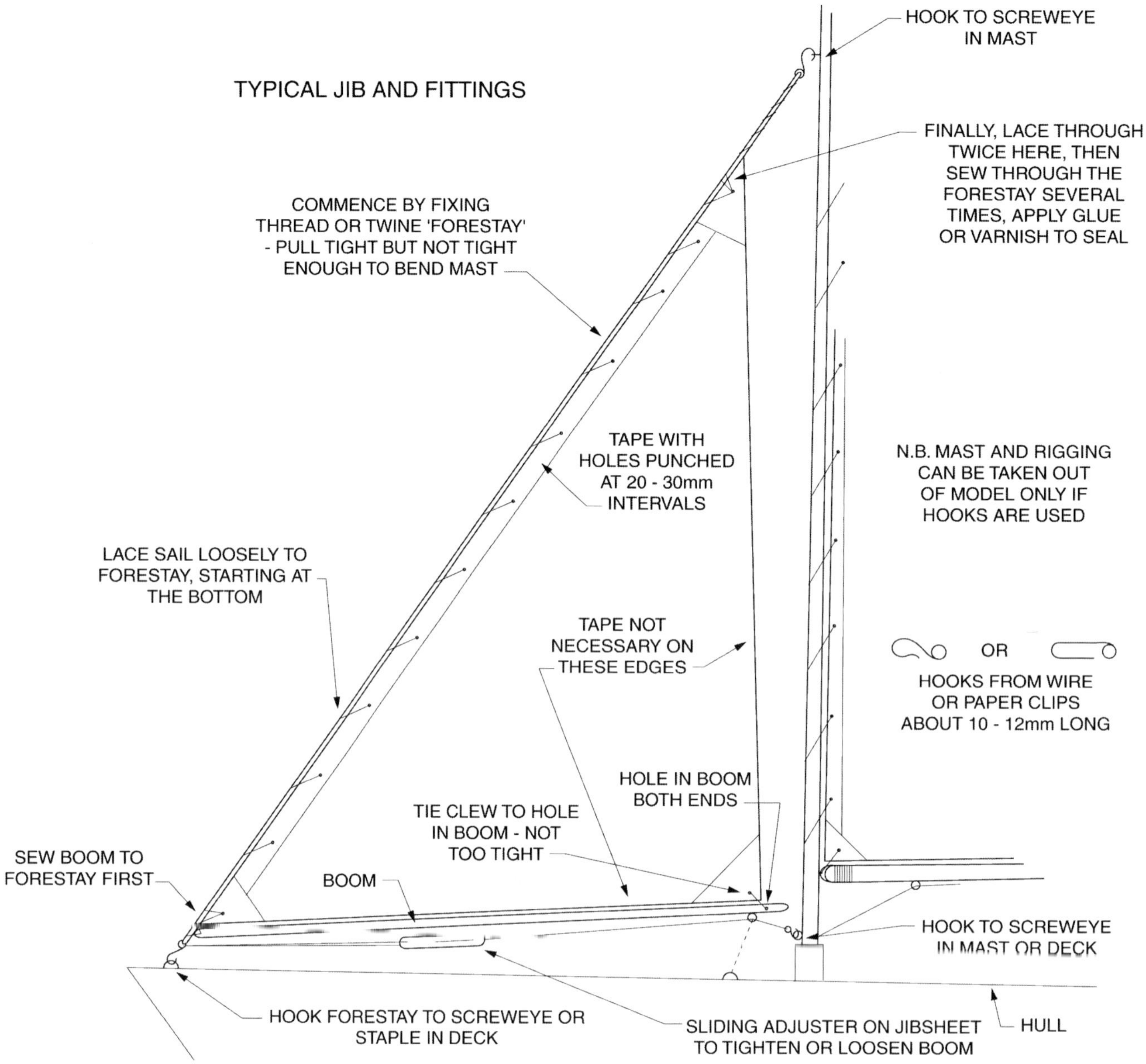

HOOK TO SCREWEYE IN MAST
FINALLY, LACE THROUGH TWICE HERE, THEN SEW THROUGH THE FORESTAY SEVERAL TIMES, APPLY GLUE OR VARNISH TO SEAL
COMMENCE BY FIXING THREAD OR TWINE 'FORESTAY' - PULL TIGHT BUT NOT TIGHT ENOUGH TO BEND MAST
TAPE WITH HOLES PUNCHED AT 20 - 30mm INTERVALS
N.B. MAST AND RIGGING CAN BE TAKEN OUT OF MODEL ONLY IF HOOKS ARE USED
LACE SAIL LOOSELY TO FORESTAY, STARTING AT THE BOTTOM
TAPE NOT NECESSARY ON THESE EDGES
OR
HOOKS FROM WIRE OR PAPER CLIPS ABOUT 10 - 12mm LONG
HOLE IN BOOM BOTH ENDS
TIE CLEW TO HOLE IN BOOM - NOT TOO TIGHT
SEW BOOM TO FORESTAY FIRST
BOOM
HOOK TO SCREWEYE IN MAST OR DECK
HOOK FORESTAY TO SCREWEYE OR STAPLE IN DECK
SLIDING ADJUSTER ON JIBSHEET TO TIGHTEN OR LOOSEN BOOM
HULL

TYPICAL SLIDING ADJUSTER MADE FROM WHITE PLASTIC

SCREWEYE IN BOOM OR DECK
ABOUT 15mm
SCREWEYE OR HOLE IN BOOM
HOOK TO DECK OR MAST

LOOSELY TAPE AT ENDS
BLOCK 10mm OR LESS
THIN STICK 6mm SQ.
THICK STICK 18mm SQ.
ABOUT 600mm

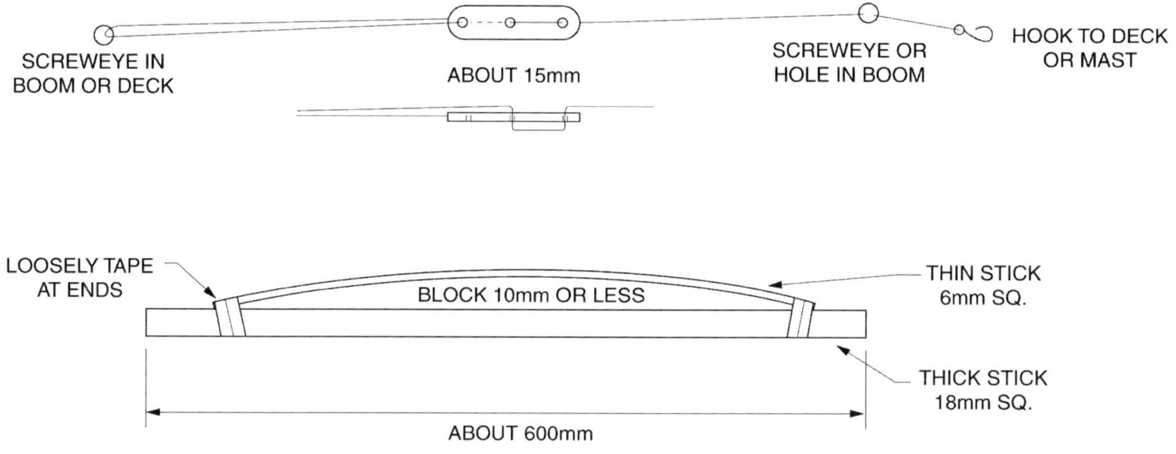

'BENT STICK' DEVICE FOR CUTTING SLIGHT CURVES ON 'TRAILING EDGE' OF MAINSAILS

models anyway, using the method described on these pages, I can do it all myself (and keep my money!).

I first used greaseproof paper on the mini tea clipper described in this book. It was so successful, I now use it on much larger models. Providing it doesn't get soaked it lasts surprisingly well. Also, making a new sail to replace a damaged one doesn't take long. Plastic sails are almost as easy to make. Bin liners or carrier bags can be used or sometimes you can buy opaque white plastic sheet used for tablecloths (from market stalls). The very light striped carrier bags are particularly good, usually red and white or blue and white stripes.

Painting

One 250ml tin of clear polyurethane varnish is more than enough to coat all the models in this book three times. For colours, you can use left-over house paint, but this often turns out to be semi-solid and full of sand. It is far better to buy small tins of *Humbrol* (or similar) enamel and get a brilliant finish. If the deck is to be left varnished, it needs three coats before you paint colour on the sides of the boat. This will prevent paint soaking into the edges of the deck. Clean paint lines are essential and to do this you must stroke the brush up towards the deck when painting which leaves a clean edge between paint and deck.

Clean brushes thoroughly immediately after use in white spirit.

Keels

Balsa at least ⅛in. (3mm) thick can be used for keels but for the majority of models 4mm or 5mm ply is better. Most of the boats in this book use fishing weights for ballast. Cutting out the shape in balsa or ply needs care, to ensure that the weight is a reasonable fit.

When using balsa, cut out undersize with a sharp Stanley knife, and file out the final shape with glasspaper wrapped round a short piece of dowel. When the weight just fits the hole, run plenty of balsa cement round both sides to fix it. If using plywood, drill out the biggest hole you can and use a file or glasspaper to get a fit. It is best to use *Araldite* to fix the weight in ply, but balsa cement will do.

Flat aluminium plate makes excellent keels as does two sheets of formica glued back to back with contact adhesive. Model making is all about improvising with whatever you can get hold of.

Most of the models in this book carry a lead weight in the keel for ballast. Long ago, I started using 'swivel bombs' used by anglers and obtainable from any fishing tackle shop. These can be obtained at almost any weight up to 8oz. A hole of the right size and shape has to be cut into the keel. In balsa, this should be cut out well undersize with a Stanley-type knife. Sandpaper wrapped round a dowel is used to open the hole out until a good fit is obtained then fasten in place with balsa cement.

In ply it is a little more difficult. A coping saw or fretsaw can be used, but simply drilling out the largest hole possible and using sandpaper until a good fit is obtained isn't too difficult. Use *Araldite* to fix.

Cardboard

This is a most useful material for modelling which can be used as cutting boards, for patterns and even for the models if well painted.

A particularly tough material is pasteboard with a shiny white surface on both sides. Mounting board, used in picture framing, has one white surface and one coloured, both types being available quite cheaply from art shops. I always cut up cereal packets too because I hate to waste anything!

Paperclips

The wire these are made from is ideal for modelling. Rigging hooks are easily made using needle-nosed pliers.

Lolly sticks

These make excellent paint-stirrers and reinforcement for balsa where required – make a point of collecting some.

Simple 9in. Sailboard

This simple model should give a lot of fun to 10 to 11 year-olds. Surfboards have proved very successful at the seaside and local ponds and they really can shift in a good wind. Four can be made from one sheet of ⅛in. (3mm) balsa 3in. × 36in. (75mm × 920mm), plus a small tube of cement, a couple of lolly sticks, cotton, paint and foil for the sails, so they are not exactly expensive!

Apart from simplicity, the main features are great stability and the scope for hull decoration, which can be as elaborate as the builder desires: teachers will appreciate this is the bit children enjoy! Several schools used this design when it was first published in *Model Boats* (April 1975) with good results as I understand.

Construction

Hull

Study the plans. From your 9in. × 3in. (920mm × 75mm) piece of balsa cut a ¼in. (6mm) strip from one long edge and put aside (this will form the mast later). Mark a line across the board 1½in. (40mm) from one end. Draw round a tin to mark the round end and remove the waste with a sharp Stanley-type knife, making sure the work is resting on a cutting board and not directly on the table or bench! Glasspaper the ends smooth. Now cut the hole for the mast as shown, right through the board. Also cut the slot for the keel about 2mm wide so the keel is a tight fit. Both these slots should be on the centre line. Cut a slit each end for the rigging as shown. Next, the nose of the boat has to be bent up. Cut along the line drawn across the board halfway through the thickness only. Break the board across this line and bend up the front. Run some balsa cement along the joint and smooth with finger. If the rounded end breaks off when you try to crack the board, cement it back on and support the raised end until dry. This joint must be strong.

Mast

From the 6mm strip originally cut from board, a 5½in. (140mm) length is required. The top end has to be narrow for 1in (25mm) as shown. Push the mast into the slot and cement securely. Ensure that the mast is upright when viewed from front and leans back towards stern slightly. Now pull cotton through the slit in the bows, pass round the mast twice on top of the 'step' then down through the slit in the stern. Pull taut and cement under each end, after snipping off all but ¼in. (6mm).

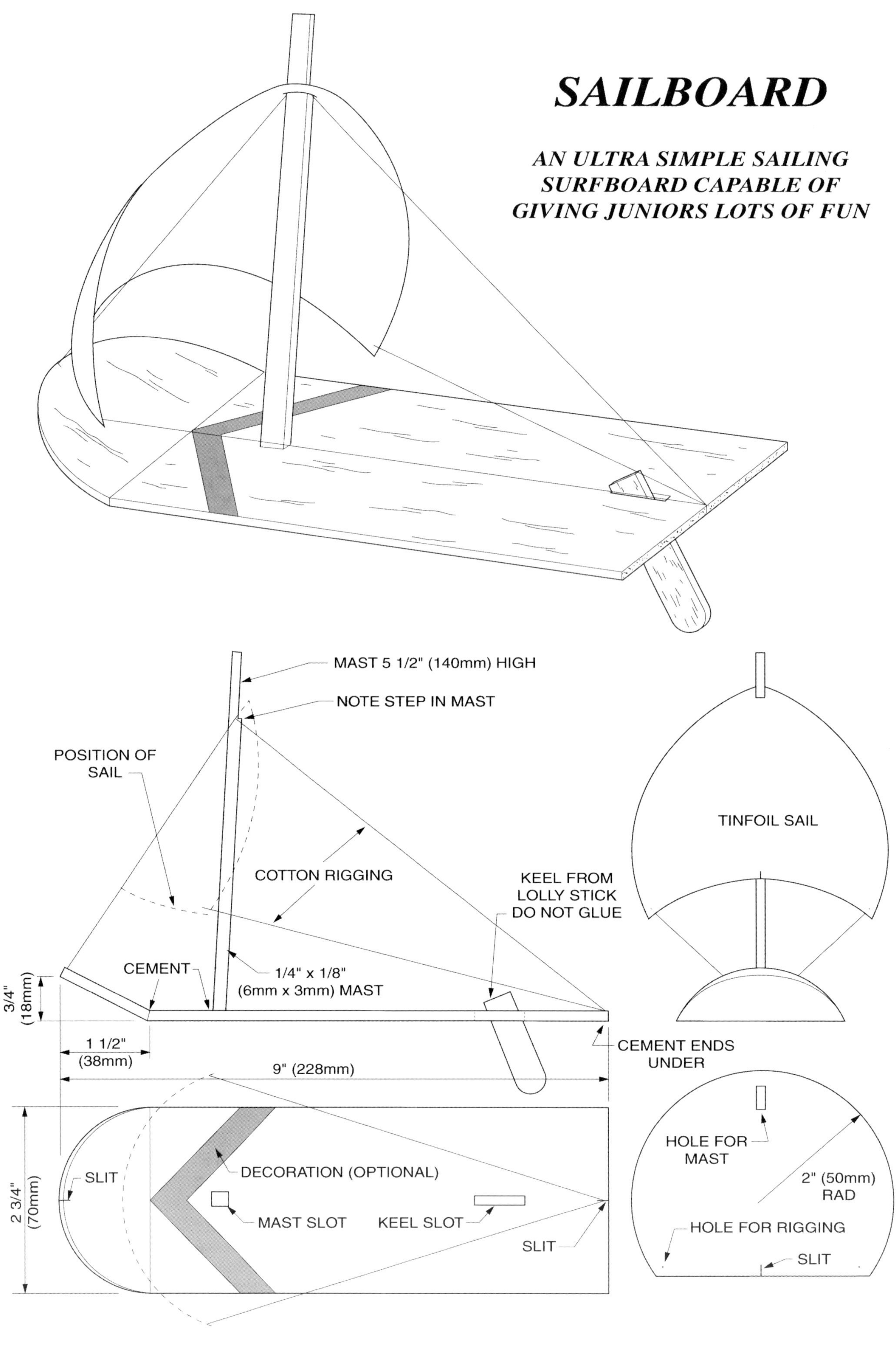
SAILBOARD
AN ULTRA SIMPLE SAILING SURFBOARD CAPABLE OF GIVING JUNIORS LOTS OF FUN
MAST 5 1/2" (140mm) HIGH
NOTE STEP IN MAST
POSITION OF SAIL
TINFOIL SAIL
COTTON RIGGING
KEEL FROM LOLLY STICK DO NOT GLUE
CEMENT
1/4" x 1/8" (6mm x 3mm) MAST
3/4" (18mm)
1 1/2" (38mm)
CEMENT ENDS UNDER
9" (228mm)
HOLE FOR MAST
2 3/4" (70mm)
SLIT
DECORATION (OPTIONAL)
2" (50mm) RAD
MAST SLOT
KEEL SLOT
HOLE FOR RIGGING
SLIT
SLIT

Painting

The hull is now complete and can be decorated – you can let loose your artistic talents! First, it is best to give the whole boat a coat of varnish or sanding sealer to seal the wood then hang the boat up to dry. When dry the main colour can be applied all over. Any paint can be used (even emulsion) but, of course, the more glossy the finish, the faster the boat will go. At least two coats of the main colour should be given and any decoration you fancy put on in a different colour. The simplest is a broad arrowhead as shown on the drawing, but do whatever you like. If you really want class, think of a name and paint it on or use transfers.

Sails

Paper is useless if it gets wet so I don't recommend it. Take an aluminium foil pie or cake case and cut out a 4in. (100mm) diameter circle. Cut off the bottom 1in. (25mm) as shown so you have a shape resembling a setting sun. Cut a small slit in the centre of the straight edge. At each corner poke a small hole and tie a piece of cotton about 9in. (230mm) long. Cut a small hole in the top centre of sail and push the sail down onto the mast as far as the step. Pull the cotton rigging through the slit in the stem and draw tight until the sail is evenly curved. Cement the ends under as before. The cotton in front of the mast should rest in the slit in the bottom edge of the sail. I have recently discovered that large waxed paper cups can be used for sails, as the photographs demonstrate.

Keel

This is simply a 2in. (50mm) length of lolly stick pushed through the slit cut for it. It is only necessary to put the keel in when the boat is being sailed, otherwise the boat can stand on any surface to be admired.

Sailing

Any clear stretch of water will do. Note which way the wind is blowing and place the boat in the water with the wind behind it. Two or more boats will make a real race of it. If the wind is very strong or changes direction quickly the boat may capsize. This will not matter too much as the sail is waterproof and the boat cannot sink. Have fun!

A 22in. Windsurfer

You can build this simple sailing surfboard, a development of the smaller surfboard that appeared in *Model Boats* (April 1975), from two sheets of balsa. The little ones scoot downwind like lightning in a breeze, but have to be lifted out of the water at the end of each run. This larger version is almost as easy to make but has a weighted keel and a conventional sailplan so that it will tack across the wind as a yacht should.

Two of these attractive craft can be made from one sheet of ¼in. (6mm) balsa plus one sheet of ⅛in. (3mm), both 3in. (75mm) wide by 36in. (920mm) long. Other materials needed are one ¼in. (6mm) dowel 36in. long, two 2½ oz swivel-bomb fishing lead weights, a small tube of balsa cement, thread, polythene bag for sails and paper-clips.

Construction

Take an 18in. (460mm) piece of balsa ¼in. (6mm) thick by 3in. (75mm) wide. Mark a line along the centre of the board. Carefully check the plan for measurements and mark out the slots for keel and rudder. These should be slightly less than 3mm wide. It is a good idea to mark out on both sides of the board. Cut out the slots with a sharp modelling knife from both sides, so that they are square through the board. The keel is not glued into the slot, therefore it should be a nice tight fit. The same applies to the rudder. If you do make the slots too wide, the keel and rudder can be glued in, but they are supposed to be adjustable – and removable.

Right, we have the slots cut so on to the next bit, the raised nose. From the 3mm thick balsa sheet, cut off a piece 3in. (75mm) long. One end has to be shaped into a semi-circle. Draw round a tin to get a perfect half-round shape, cut off the waste and sand smooth. Now chamfer the front end of the main board until the nose makes a nice shallow angle. Glue in place and hold with a couple of pins until set. It will now be necessary to sand the joint flush at the bottom (see inset on drawing). Also sand a radius on the stern as shown.

The next item is the mast step. Shape a piece of 3mm balsa into a long egg shape and glue into position on the centre line of the deck. A hole, ¼in. (6mm) is drilled through this for the mast to stand in. You can twirl a drill in your fingers as the balsa is so soft but do not go right through the bottom – about 6mm deep is fine.

The mast is made from 6mm dowel, 18in. long, tapered at the top. Drill a fine hole near to the top and fix the screweye or split pin at the lower end for the boom fixing as described earlier. Make the boom from dowel 8½in. (215mm) long. Fix a screweye for the main 'sheet' which controls the angle of the sail, and drill a fine hole near the outer end to attach the sail itself.

Attach the boom to the mast before setting the mast up. Glue the mast into the step, making sure it is upright when viewed from the front and leans back slightly towards the stern.

Now for the rigging, which has been kept as simple as possible. Thread a darning needle with carpet thread and push it right through the hull bottom just behind the nose. Pull about 3 feet (1 metre) through. Snip off about ½in. (12mm) below the hull bottom. Smear a little balsa cement behind the hole and stick the thread to the wood. When dry, take the thread up to the top of the mast and wind two turns around (do not overtighten), and back through one of the slits in the stern. Pull taut, snip off and cement end under as before. Now attach a thread from the top of the mast to the slit in the other side.

Both backstays (as they are called) should be evenly taut and the mast must be upright when viewed from the front. A little balsa cement smeared on the turns at the masthead will stop anything slipping.

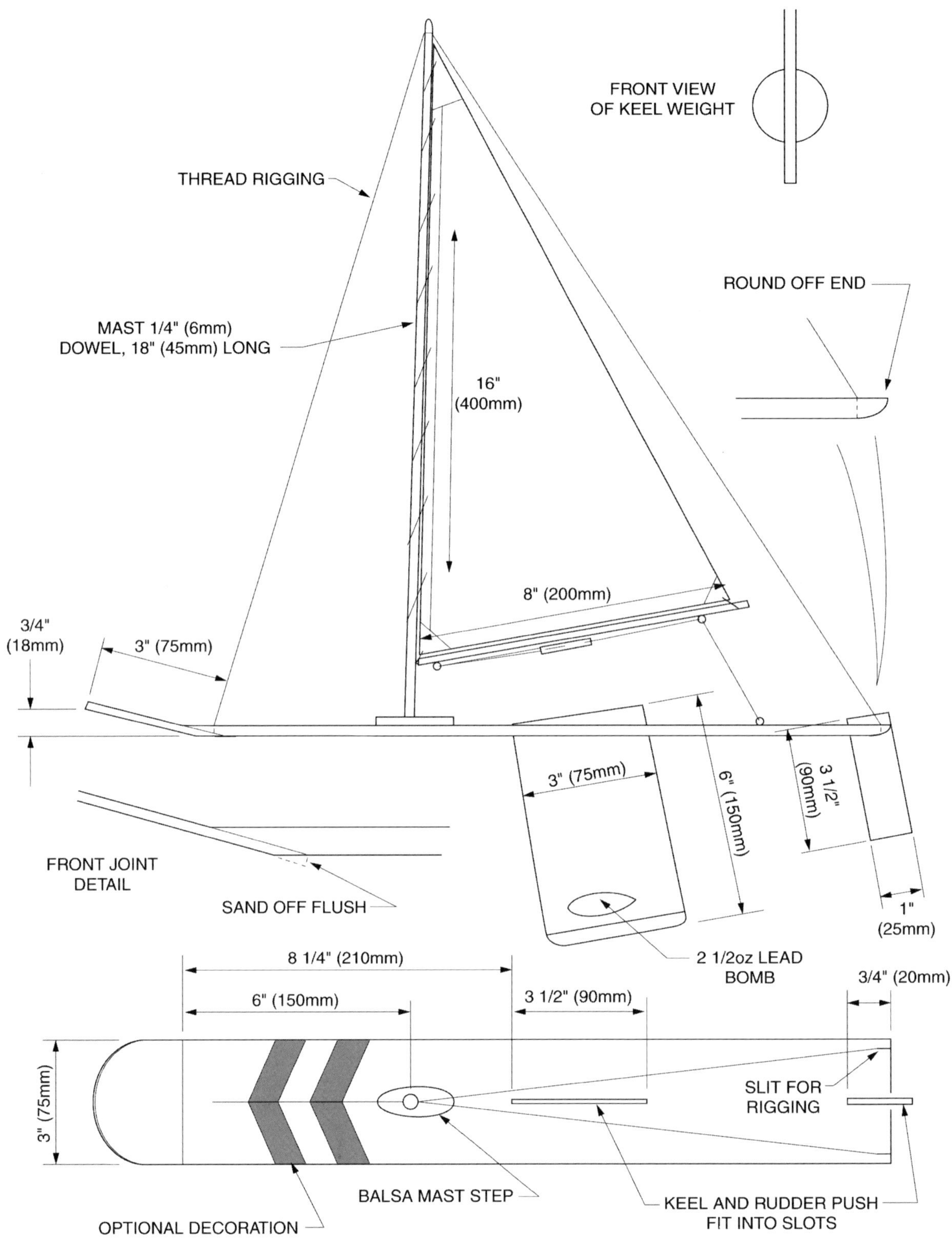

Keel

This is made from ⅛in. (3mm) balsa, and should be 6in. (150mm) long when finished. It is a good idea to cement a strip across the grain at the bottom as shown on the drawing, which will help stop the keel from warping. This strip should be ½in. (12mm) wide. Sand all the edges round to streamline the board.

Now the swivel-bomb fishing lead has to be set into the keel. Snip off the brass swivel and draw round the weight onto the keel. A neat fit is required so cut out the shape undersize to start with. Enlarge it with a piece of sandpaper rolled round a pencil until the weight just fits. Run some balsa cement round both sides and smooth with a finger. You may have to add more balsa cement to fill any large gaps.

Make the rudder from ⅛in. (3mm) balsa also. Both the keel and rudder should be a push fit on the slots.

After checking all the items for alignment, separate them and give them all a coat of clear varnish or sanding sealer. When dry – not before – paint the main colour all over the hull and hang it up to dry by the mast.

Decoration can be added in a different colour according to your taste. The original is white with red and blue stripes, the keel and rudder being red – very smart! A yellow hull with black decoration looks good also.

Sail

While the paint is drying the sail can be made. Refer to the notes on making sails earlier (see page 2). The choice of using polythene or greaseproof paper is up to you.

Remember, a well-made sail which sets well (no creases) makes all the difference to a sailing boat's performance, even a simple one like this. Make sure the thread that 'laces' the sail to the mast is not pulled too tight, otherwise it will not be able to swing from side to side without jamming. Fit a sliding adjuster to the boom so that the angle of the sail can be varied.

Sailing

When the great day comes for sailing trials a lot can be learned about the way sailboats work from watching this one.

Let the sail out about halfway, angle the keel and rudder as shown on the plan and set sail. Watch carefully. If all is well she will keep a pretty straight course, even if she is well heeled over. However, if she tries to turn away from the wind the keel is too far back. Standing it more upright in the slot should improve matters. Should she try to head up into the wind, moving the keel back will help.

A real windsurfer can alter his course by moving the sail forward or back, or by shifting his weight. We can't do that so easily with our model, but it is possible to observe how different set-ups can affect performance. If several of these little boats are on the water at the same time it gives all the ingredients for racing and a good time should be had by all.

Note: this model first appeared as an article in *Model Boats* December 1977. The text has been revised to include metric measurement but the boat is the same.

Mini Tea Clipper

One of the most beautiful of man's creations must be the fast sailing ships built in the latter half of the last century. They were the result of many years of experiment and development with one objective in mind – speed.

What a sight they must have been, roaring along with a great bone of foam slicing the bows and vast pyramids of straining canvas. Alas, it is a sight no longer to be seen, but the fascination lives on and modelling a square-rigger is a most rewarding project. This model is of the earlier type of wooden clipper which carried fewer sails and would be about 190ft (60 metres) long. The scale is approximately 12 feet to the inch (a man would be about ½in. or 12mm tall!).

I have attempted to simplify this design as much as possible while, at the same time, retaining some of the grace of the full-sized ship. Extra detail such as guard rails, boats etc. can be added as desired.

Although a square-rigger is extremely complicated, this model is quite easy to make. One of the prime objectives was a model ship which could be converted from a charming ornament for the mantelpiece to a sailing model by the simple attachment of a false keel. It appears to do both things very well.

Construction

Hull

The hull is made from a 16in. (410mm) length of 2in. × 1in. (50mm × 25mm) softwood. The actual size of planed timber will be a little less than 2in. × 1in. This should be marked out as per the plan, taking great care to get both sides the same. A cardboard pattern for the bows will help here.

Before shaping starts, make a saw-cut across one end of the timber. This is to hold the cutwater later. Shape the hull with a plane or a sharp knife and sand carefully. Note that it is important to leave the edges square – do not attempt to round them off top or bottom. The hull is slightly flared at the bows i.e. the deck is less pointed than the underside of the hull.

The stern is slightly rounded in profile (see plan). No attempt has been made to shape the afterbody into the complicated hollow section that it should be, for reasons of simplicity – at least, that's my excuse! When you are satisfied the hull is nicely shaped, the balsa deck can be added.

First, a short piece of balsa wood ¼in. (6mm) thick is glued onto the bows covering the cutwater slot. A further piece of balsa ⅛in. (3mm) thick is

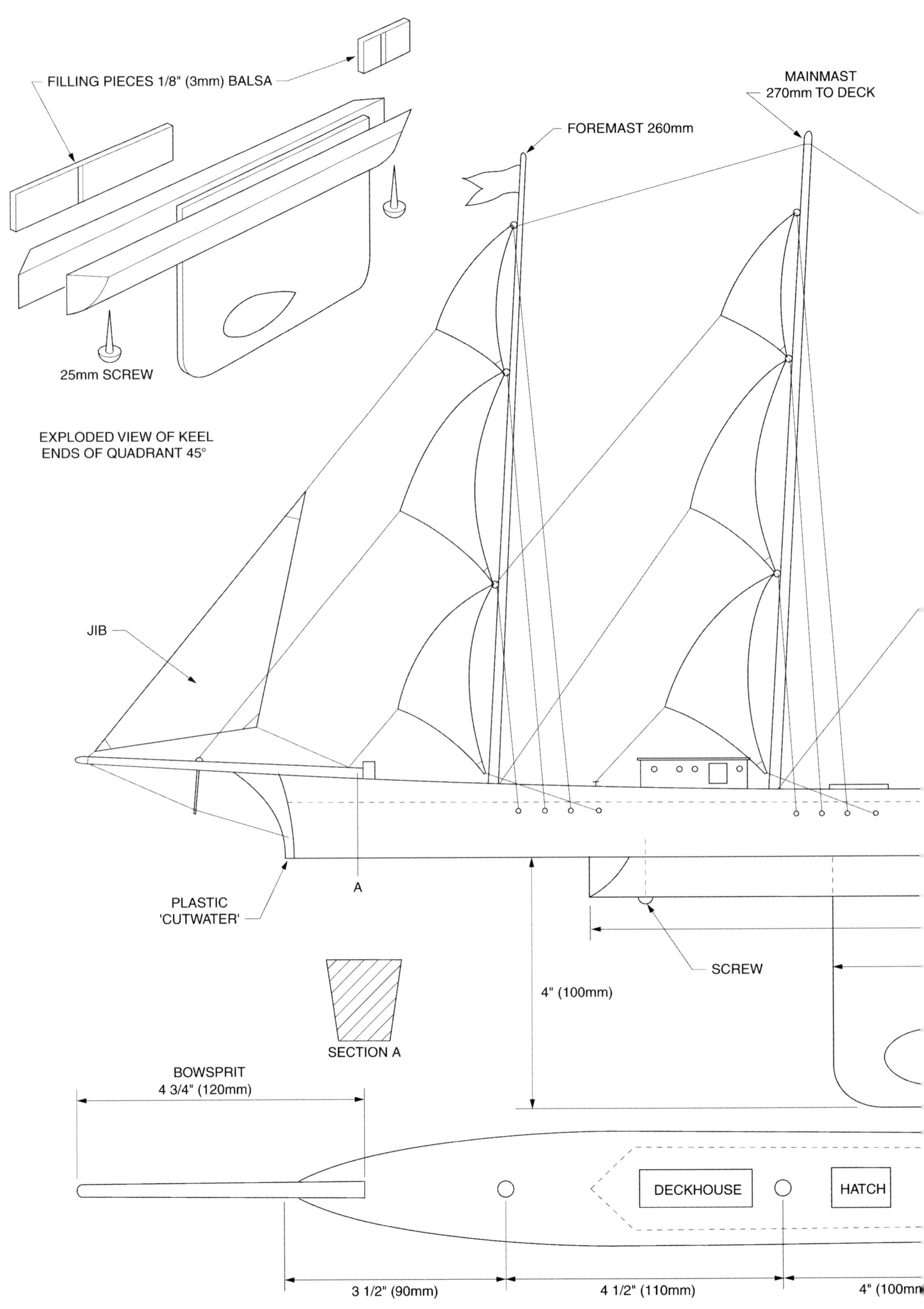
FILLING PIECES 1/8" (3mm) BALSA
25mm SCREW
EXPLODED VIEW OF KEEL
ENDS OF QUADRANT 45°
MAINMAST
270mm TO DECK
FOREMAST 260mm
JIB
PLASTIC
'CUTWATER'
A
SCREW
4" (100mm)
SECTION A
BOWSPRIT
4 3/4" (120mm)
DECKHOUSE
HATCH
3 1/2" (90mm)
4 1/2" (110mm)
4" (100mm

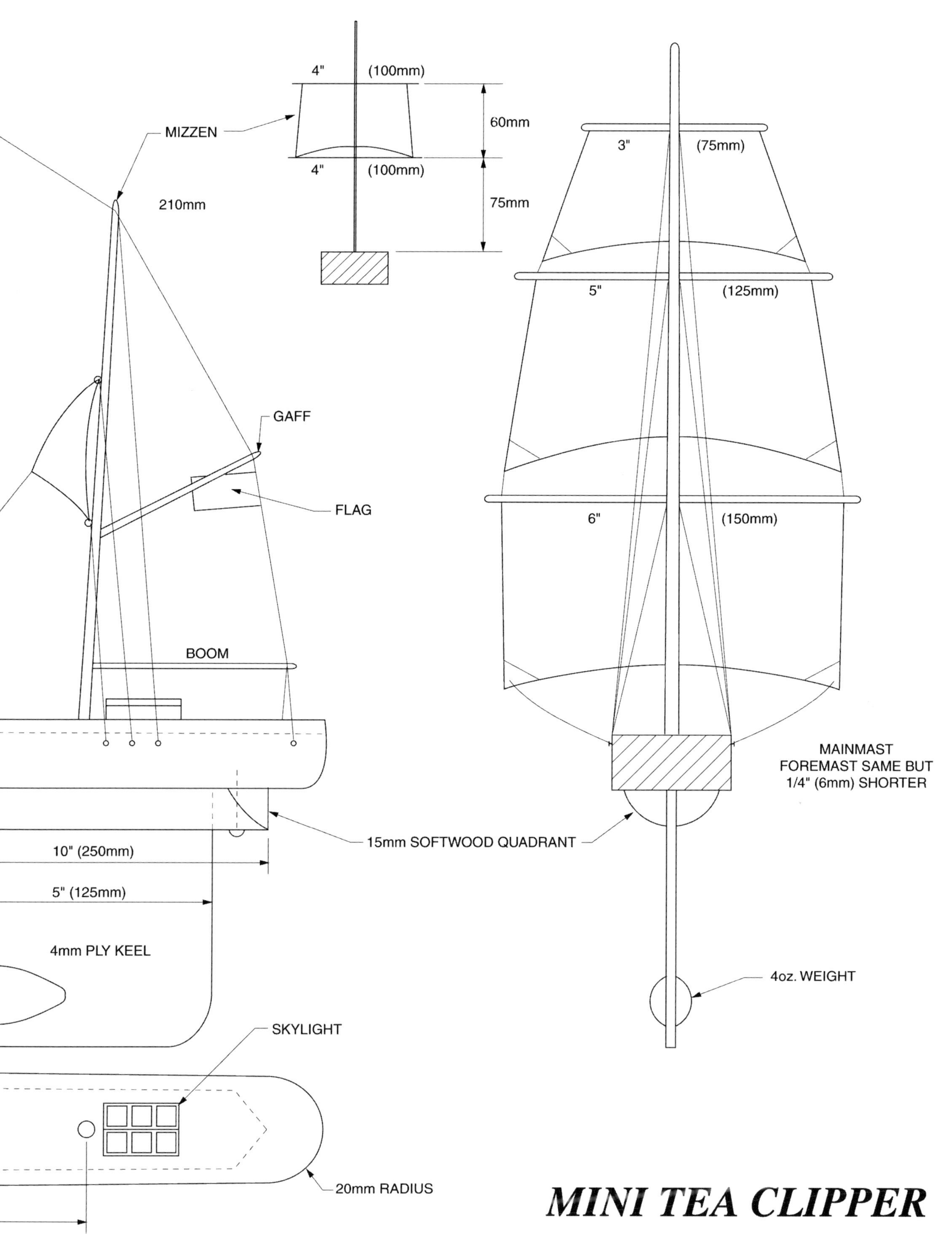

MINI TEA CLIPPER

glued onto the stern. The deck is 3mm balsa, big enough to cover the entire hull. Spread plenty of PVA glue over the underside of the deck and stick down. Place a heavy object (such as an electric iron) on the centre of the deck to hold it down while the glue sets. You can wrap tape round the middle of the hull instead of using weights. Whatever you use, make sure the deck doesn't slip to one side before the glue dries!

Shape the deck to conform with the main hull. The deck should now have a nice 'sheer' caused by the wedges at both ends. Fill in the gaps along the sides with scrap balsa and sand to a nice, smooth finish. Finally, plaster can be used to fill small cracks etc.

Run the blade of a saw through the cutwater slot so that the slot extends right up to deck level. Make the bowsprit from dowel or cane complete with 'dolphin striker' made from a ¾in. (20mm) panel pin. Glue and pin it onto the deck. The cutwater can now be made and pushed into the slot. Plastic or very thin plywood can be used for this.

Drill the small hole before fitting. The cutwater, or stem, to give it the correct name, is a very important part of the ship. It should be carefully shaped and fitted tight up under the bowsprit. As soon as it is in place, the whole graceful impression of a sailing ship magically appears.

At this stage, a sealing coat of clear varnish can be given all over the hull. Drill holes for masts to suit the dowel size, probably 3⁄16in. (4mm) and remember that the masts are raked backwards slightly. If you have access to a pillar drill, place a 1in. (25mm) block under the stern to get all the masts at the same angle.

Mark points at which small gimp pins are to be driven into hull sides for attaching rigging. Gimp pins are like small tin tacks, however, you could use small brass flat-headed pins instead. Leave the heads sticking out a little until the rigging has been attached.

Add deckhouse, skylight, hatch etc. to the deck and paint to taste, probably black hull, clear varnished deck, white deckhouse, skylight. The skylight has black windows painted on, a nice touch worth the extra care. A very thin gold or white stripe right round the hull just below the nails adds much to the overall appearance if it is carefully done. The best results are obtained using pinstripe tape available from auto accessory shops.

Masts and spars

Dowel used for masts and spars is 3⁄16in. (4mm) although ⅛in. (3mm) for the upper spars would look better if available. Again, for simplicity, masts are one piece instead of three.

Cut the masts to length and taper the top section. It is possible to use a small piece of broken window glass as a scraper. Glass makes an excellent scraper but, of course, you must be careful not to cut yourself so wear a glove. **Note: not for children, please**.

Simply using sandpaper, while rotating the dowel with your fingers, will soon result in a gradual taper. Cut all the spars to length and taper the end sections. Lay the spars on a piece of lined paper with the mast laying on top. Glue the mast and spars together using a hefty blob of glue at each joint. The lined paper will help to keep everything square. Waterproof glue such as PVA, resin W or balsa cement should be used throughout.

Obviously, all the joints must be strong – if in doubt bind with cotton. In the case of the mizzen mast, glue the boom and gaff first. When these joints are firmly set, glue the spars.

Do not, on any account, move any of the masts until the glue holding the spars on is properly set, say 24 hours. If you do, the yards may droop or fall off which is definitely bad news.

Varnish all masts and yards and leave to dry.

Rigging

Patience is required for rigging this ship and you will probably discover that you have fingers like bananas. Don't rush, think about the next stage before you do it and it will be quite easy – well, fairly easy.

Commence with the mizzen mast first and work forward. The best thing to use for rigging is black carpet thread, which can usually be bought at a shoe repair shop. Shrouds (the ropes that support the mast from the sides) are attached as follows.

Tie thread to the nail nearest the mast on the ship's side. Pass the end round the mast above the lowest spar. Take it down to the nail on the opposite side and back along to the next nail. Up again to the next spar and so on until all the spars and nails are occupied.

Do not overtighten the thread. Make sure the mast is upright when viewed from the front. Tie the thread onto the last nail and push the nails in a little more. A touch of glue or varnish in all the knots will hold everything secure.

The mainmast and the foremast can now be rigged in the same way. Remember, before you push these masts into their holes, to put a long piece of thread under them. These threads (called stays) run up to one of the upper yards on the next mast aft and are quite important (time to look at the plans again).

There are a couple more stays to fit. A small brass nail or gimp pin should be tapped into the deck just in front of the deckhouse. Tie a thread to that and run it up to the lowest yard on the mainmast. Tie it round the mast just above the yard.

The next stay runs from a nail almost at the inboard end of the bowsprit and straight up to the top yard on the mainmast, passing under the yard on the foremast as it goes. Another stay is tied round the bowsprit at the dolphin striker and up to the middle yard on the foremast. The last one is a long one. It is first tied to the hole in the cutwater. Take a couple of turns round the bottom end of the dolphin striker, then a couple more round the end of the bowsprit. From there, up to the top yard on the foremast, take a turn round the mast and across to the next and so on until you reach the end of the boom. Tie it off there. A short length of thread tied to the nail on each side of the stern to hold the boom down completes the rigging. All the knots should now be glued or varnished and the loose ends snipped off. If you haven't gone grey by now, the sails can be added. Good quality greaseproof paper can be used for the sails. On the original model these have proved quite satisfactory.

Each sail is cut to shape and a length of cotton tied to the bottom corners, before the sail is glued to its spar. The bottom corners of all sails are best reinforced with masking tape. Start with the lower sails first and work up. The sail is glued along the top of the spar so that it flies well out (PVA glue is best as it dries clear).

Note that each sail is above a stay which runs down to the next mast forward. When the corners of the sail are pulled back and attached by the cotton sheets to the spar below, the sail will take up a lovely curve. The stay holds the belly of the sail out as though the wind is filling it.

Once the first sail is done the rest are easy. Really!

The jib sail is best laced onto the forestay with needle and cotton although glue will do. There is no 'spanker' sail set on the mizzen, as this would prevent the ship running downwind.

Keel

Notes on the detachable keel have been left until last, but this part should be made and fitted to the hull before the masts and rigging are done. It can then be detached and left aside until the ship is complete.

The keel is a sheet of balsa or ply about ⅛in. (3mm) thick sandwiched between two lengths of softwood quadrant (see drawing for dimensions). The ballast is provided by a 4oz swivel-bomb fishing weight let into the keel. Nip off the swivel and draw the outline of the bomb onto the keel as shown. The hole must be carefully cut and sanded until the weight just pushes in tight. Balsa cement run round the edges of the weight each side will hold it in place. Paint the keel a dark colour all over so it will not be obvious when afloat.

Sailing

The model will only run downwind so place it in the water with the wind behind it and let go. As she accelerates away you can spend a moment or two admiring your handiwork – but don't stand too long or she'll be across to the other side before you. That's the keep fit part!

Note: a national flag flying just below the gaff provides a perfect finishing touch. Draw your flag 1in. × ½in. (25mm × 12mm) on fine white paper on both sides using a ballpoint pen. Scrunch it up a bit, flatten out and glue to the thread – flying forward please.

Seacat – A 24in. (610mm) Easy-build Catamaran

Seacat is suitable as a school project for children aged 12 years or over, and may perhaps appeal to all those fathers who get asked "Make me a boat, Dad" and who have never made a boat before.

This lively catamaran is easily constructed from readily available materials, and will cost very little. Catamarans are fast and simply made but they do suffer certain disadvantages. First, if overcanvassed they will flip over and, secondly, they can bury the lee bow and nosedive.

However, *Seacat* has been carefully designed and tested to overcome these faults as far as possible. If built as shown she will perform very well.

The hulls only take 15 minutes or so each to make and the whole ship no more than three or four hours (not allowing for the time paint takes to dry!). The sails are the most difficult part to make but, usually, a kind person can be persuaded to 'run up' these on a sewing machine if the right approach is made. If not, perfectly good sails can be made from polythene, as already described.

Construction

Hulls

Two pieces of clean softwood 2in. × 1in. (50mm × 25mm) planed are required, each 24in. (610mm) long. Actually, the timber will be a little thinner – about 45mm × 22mm. If there are knots in the wood, try to keep them away from the ends. Cut one end to an angle of 45 degrees and the other end at about 15 degrees as shown on the plan.

Each end should be sanded to a nice round section. When both ends are shaped, make a mark ½in. (12mm) up from the bottom at the bows (front end!) with a pencil. Plane the bottom in a nice curve to meet this mark, both hulls to be the same, of course. The stern end is just slightly rounded off as shown. Now sand the hulls all over to a smooth finish.

For the crossbeams, two pieces of 1in. × ¼in. (25mm by 6mm) timber are needed. Ramin was used on the original but ordinary laths would be

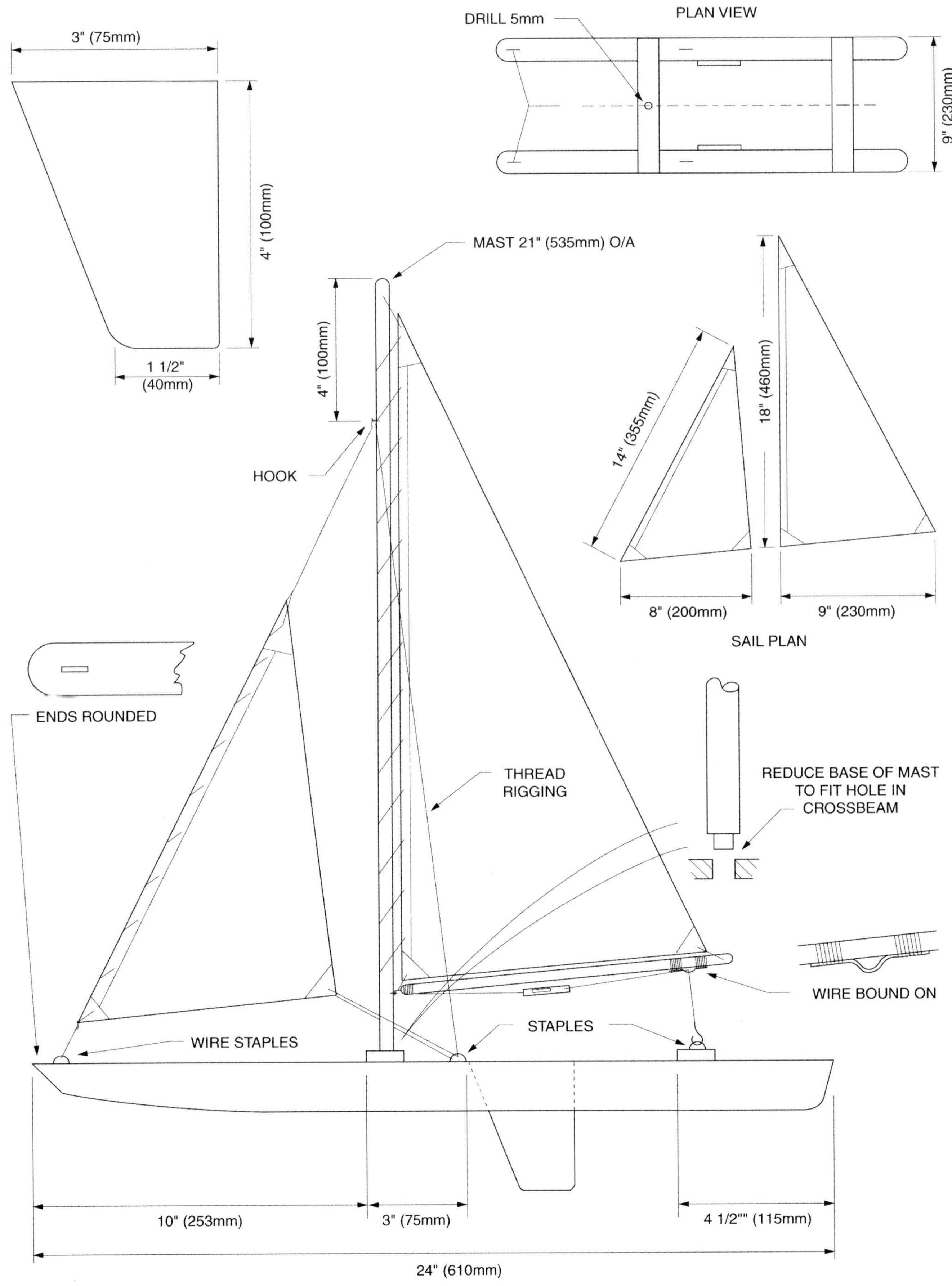

3" (75mm)
4" (100mm)
1 1/2"
(40mm)
DRILL 5mm
PLAN VIEW
9" (230mm)
MAST 21" (535mm) O/A
4" (100mm)
HOOK
14" (355mm)
18" (460mm)
8" (200mm)
9" (230mm)
SAIL PLAN
ENDS ROUNDED
THREAD
RIGGING
REDUCE BASE OF MAST
TO FIT HOLE IN
CROSSBEAM
WIRE BOUND ON
WIRE STAPLES
STAPLES
10" (253mm)
3" (75mm)
4 1/2"" (115mm)
24" (610mm)

suitable. Cut these to a length of 9in. (230mm) and sand smooth. Place hulls of a flat surface 9in. apart, glue and pin crossbeams onto the hulls as shown, making sure that they are placed as per the plan and all is square. Leave until the glue is set.

A hole, 4mm or 5mm, should be drilled in the centre of the forward crossbeam to take the mast before assembly. When the glue is dry, tap in four small staples, two in each hull, to take the rigging. Small screweyes could be used instead of staples but they must be placed as shown.

The next items required are the two keel plates, which can be cut from hardboard or ⅛in. (3mm) ply. Simply sand the edges smooth and round off. Please note that if hardboard is being used make sure the plates are a pair, i.e. mark out back to back on the smooth surface otherwise you will have one smooth side and one rough side showing. If you do it incorrectly you will see what I mean! Glue the plates on the inside faces of the hulls exactly as shown and leave to dry. One or two small panel pins may also be used to hold them in place as well as the glue. Give the whole boat a coat of clear varnish.

When that is dry give the hulls a coat of undercoat suitable for the chosen final colour. It is a good idea to have the crossbeams left in clear varnish or painted a different colour, so bear this in mind when undercoating. Sand the hull slightly with very fine glasspaper and dust off with a clean rag before applying the final gloss coat. Take care to avoid runs in the paint by lightly brushing them away as you work. Hold the boat by the crossbeams in the last stages of painting. Hang it up to dry so that the wet paint isn't touching anything. A careful paint job makes all the difference. A name can be applied with transfers or stick-on letters. Varnish over this to waterproof.

Mast and rigging

The mast is 21in. (535mm) long and made from 6mm or 8mm dowel (preferably 8mm) with the top half tapered slightly for aesthetic reasons.

Drill a small hole near the top and fix a staple or screweye 4in. (100mm) down from the top as shown. Reduce the bottom 6mm so that it fits into the hole in the forward crossbeam. The boom is next, 10in. (250mm) long from 6mm or 8mm dowel (preferably 6mm). Drill a fine hole near the end and tape on a wire loop, or fix a screweye as shown.

Fit the boom to the mast as shown earlier. We are now ready to fit the rigging, which should be fine string or carpet twine. Knot a small loop in an 18in. (450mm) length of twine. Pass the ends through the staples in the bows and tie tight so that the loop is in the centre between the bows. This line is called the bridle.

Next, take a piece of twine about 3ft (1 metre) long and tie it round the mast above the top screweye. Stand the mast up in its hole and loosely tie the ends to the staples either side. Do not tighten the knots yet. Tie a line from the loop in the bridle up to the screweye in the upper mast. This line should have a hook at the top end so that the mast can be lowered for storage. Pull all lines tight, making sure that the mast is upright when viewed from the front and sides. Tie off permanently. Varnish the mast and boom as well as all knots to seal.

Sails

If you have chosen to have fabric sails, cut out paper patterns as per the plan and machine them from any light material such as cotton, nylon etc. I should stress that the patterns are the finished size and allowance should be made for hems. The after (back) edges of the sails should be parallel to the selvedge. Alternatively you can make the sails using plastic as described earlier. Greaseproof paper is not recommended for this boat – the sails get wet too often.

Attach the mainsail to the mast following the directions. Fit the 'sheet' which controls the boom with a sliding adjuster and hook it on to a screweye or staple fixed in the centre of the rear crossbeams.

Sew the jib sail onto the forestay as shown in the plan.

To control the jib a line is passed through a hole punched into the bottom corner of the sail (clew). The length of this line allows the jib to be set at various angles so it should also have a sliding adjuster. One end of this line (foresheet) is tied to a staple, and the other end passed through the staple on the opposite side, then back to the adjuster. This type of control eliminates the need for a boom along the bottom of the jib. Take the boat outside into the wind and make sure both sails can swing across without jamming.

Sailing

Usually, a catamaran flips over if the wind overpowers it and a capsized 'cat' cannot right itself. However, *Seacat* is different! If the wind gusts too much the leeward hull submerges. When the wind eases up it pops again and the boat sails on. Magic! Capsizes are fairly rare.

So there she is – *Seacat*. Simple, fast and cheap to make. The kids will love her, particularly if there are several to race. May she keep you quiet for a few hours' building and give you many hours of sailing pleasure.

A 'J' Class Sloop

The huge 'J' class sloops that the super-rich used to race in the 1920s and 1930s were the ultimate sailing machines. Names like *Endeavour*, *Shamrock* and *Britannia* will live forever in maritime history.

This 'J' class simple balsa sloop is a good model for a beginner to try. She sails well and has been designed with easy-build in mind. Study the plans, and try to visualise each stage as it progresses.

Construction

First, cut the sides from 3⁄32in. (2.5mm) balsa and chamfer the ends of the inside faces as shown on the drawing. Mark the position of the frames, also on the inside faces. Next, cut the frames 1, 2 and 3 exactly to the sizes given and mark the centre line on both faces. Mark a further line each side of the centre 3mm from it. Pin and glue the middle frame (no 2) into place with pins and balsa cement. When dry, pull the sides together at the ends and hold in place with masking tape. Spring frames 1 and 3 into place and secure them with pins. This will put considerable strain on the ends, so make sure that they stay closed up with more tape and pins. When you are sure that everything is in position run a line of cement down both sides of each frame and plenty into the joints at bow and stern. Leave until completely dry – four hours at least.

You will note that the straight-edged sides have now assumed a most attractive boat shape, with the ends nicely curved up. However careful you have been, it may be the sides have not bent quite the same and the boat is slightly odd in shape. Do not worry. Follow the method described next for fitting the bottom and the hull will straighten up beautifully.

Cut along the centre line of 4in. (100mm) wide 2.5mm balsa. Place the two outside (machine-cut) edges together and mark them to identify them as centre edges. Pin one piece along the bottom of the hull touching each frame on the centre line. Also line up the bow and stern with the bottom plank and pin in place. Do not glue. Now pin the other bottom plank on. Look inside the hull – is everything lined up? If so, run a ballpoint pen round the sides to mark out the bottom pieces. Also, mark the position of the frames inside the hull.

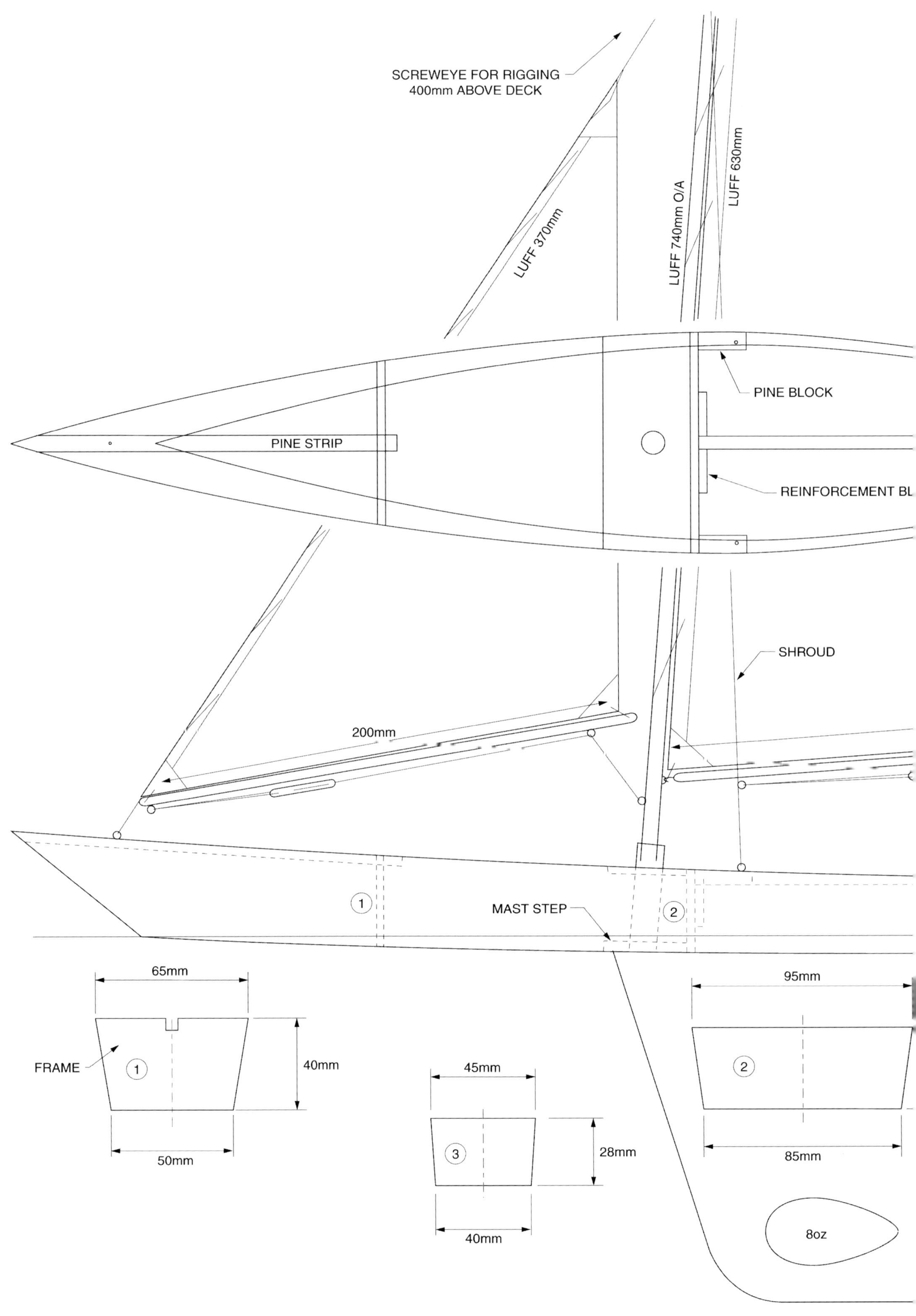

SCREWEYE FOR RIGGING
400mm ABOVE DECK
LUFF 370mm
LUFF 740mm O/A
LUFF 630mm
PINE STRIP
PINE BLOCK
REINFORCEMENT BL
SHROUD
200mm
1
MAST STEP
2
65mm
FRAME
1
40mm
50mm
45mm
3
28mm
40mm
95mm
2
85mm
8oz

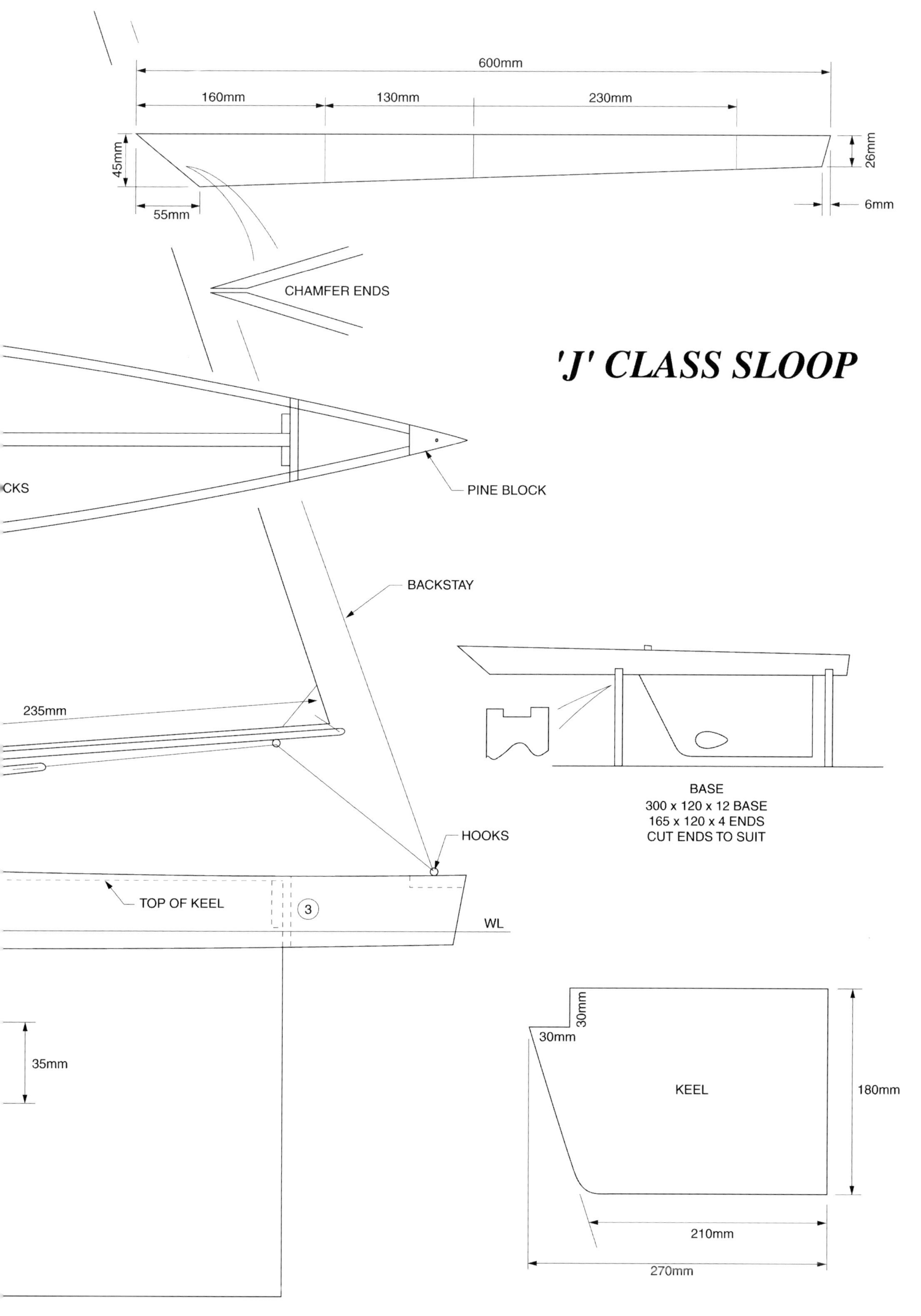

600mm
160mm
130mm
230mm
45mm
26mm
55mm
6mm
CHAMFER ENDS
'J' CLASS SLOOP
CKS
PINE BLOCK
BACKSTAY
235mm
BASE
300 x 120 x 12 BASE
165 x 120 x 4 ENDS
CUT ENDS TO SUIT
HOOKS
TOP OF KEEL
3
WL
30mm
30mm
35mm
KEEL
180mm
210mm
270mm

Remove the pins and cut out the bottom panels 2mm oversize. Now cut out the slot for the keel, between frames 2 and 3 only. This will be 2mm from each side if 4mm ply is being used for the keel.

Replace bottom panels exactly and cement in place. Use pins and tape until the cement is completely dry. When it is, remove the pins and, very carefully, sand off the surplus balsa from the bottom panels. Please note, it is easy to damage the balsa sides doing this so a good idea is to stick sandpaper to a block of wood for better control.

Make the keel from flat 4mm or 5mm ply, round off the edges and sand smooth. Cut out and shape the hole to accept an 8oz fishing weight. Cut out the shape undersize, then use sandpaper wrapped round a pencil to enlarge it until the weight fits. *Araldite* the weight in place, fill any cracks with car body filler and sand everything smooth.

Glue the keel into the hull exactly upright. This is where the lines drawn on the frames will help. Ensure the top of the keel does not project above the side panels. Fix in the holding pieces cemented to frames, either side of the keel, to reinforce it.

Hardwood blocks must now be glued in place in bow and stern to hold screweyes for the rigging before the deck goes on and also the blocks either side of the mast to hold the shrouds. (NB shrouds can be omitted.)

Make the mast tube from plastic tube cut from a felt-tip pen or ballpoint pen. This should accept 6mm dowel which is the mast diameter. Cement this securely in place set into a drilled block glued to the bottom of the hull and also through a piece set across hull at deck level.

Remember, the mast is raked back when viewed from the side and must be upright when viewed from ahead. Insert the mast while the mast tube is being fitted to help get everything lined up before the glue sets – this is important.

If satisfied that everything is glued properly and all gaps are filled, varnish the inside of the hull with clear varnish or sanding sealer. Avoid getting any on the top surfaces where the deck will have to be glued on. When dry varnish again or apply undercoat.

For the deck, cut 2.5mm balsa 4in. wide (100mm) long enough to cover the hull. Very thin marine ply can be used if preferred. Carefully mark out the hole for the mast tube, cut undersize and sand to a good fit. Tape deck in place, mark outline with ballpoint pen run round the hull. Remove the deck and cut off any surplus almost down to the outline.

Now the deck can be glued down and held with tape until the glue is dry. PVA glue will give much more time to get the deck down before the glue dries. Next, sand the edges of the deck flush with the sides. Give the deck three coats of clear varnish before painting the hull. This will prevent any paint applied to the hull from soaking into the deck. Give the hull two coats of clear varnish, one undercoat and one gloss coat, lightly sanding between each coat.

While the paint is drying the mast and rigging can be completed and the sail made. The mast and booms can be cut to length, tapered and varnished. Drill all the holes, prepare the hooks and adjusters. Attach the boom to the mast as previously described. Make the sail from plastic or grease-proof paper as preferred and complete the rigging.

This little 'J' class yacht is quite fast for her size and should last for many years if properly looked after. You may need to repaint her and renew the sails annually, but that applies to any yacht. See appendix on page 49 for imperial measurements.

Sailing

She should sail a straight course once the usual 'tuning up' has been done. Remember, if she turns up into the wind, tighten the jib in. If she turns away from the wind, tighten the mainsail or let the jib out a little.

I painted mine Oxford blue and called her *Blue-jay* – well, why not?

Swordfish – A Ketch

Swordfish is stunningly beautiful and slips along on the water very nicely too. The hull on the original is painted Oxford blue with a gold pin-stripe which makes an attractive combination.
Construction is the same as the mini tea clipper (see page 15), but the sails and rigging are probably the most difficult in this book. The small size of these items dictates that everything has to be neat and precise. A lot of patience will be required but the end result is well worth the effort.

Special points to note are as follows.

Make sure that the holes drilled for the masts are set at the required angle. The masts are raked sharply aft and they must be at the same angle. If you have a pillar drill place a 1¼in. (30mm) block under the stern. Make sure the drill does not go right through the bottom of the hull.

Cut the masts to length, remembering to add the ¾in.(18mm) extra which is glued into the hull. Taper the masts and reduce the top 6mm to form a shoulder as shown on drawing. Drill holes in the masts and booms as per the plan using either a fine watchmaker's screwdriver or 1.5mm drill before setting the masts up. Also, fix the booms to the masts before setting the masts up.

Two holes need to be drilled in the bowsprit. For the after one, twist an eye in a piece of 10 amp fuse wire, pass it through the hole and bend under before gluing the bowsprit down. You can use a small screweye, of course, if you have one. Paint the hull, varnish the deck and all spars before fixing the masts in place.

Three small staples are required – these can be cut from paperclips. Set them into the deck as shown on drawing. It is helpful to drill very fine holes to set them into, or the balsa deck may be damaged. Each sail needs a line with a sliding adjuster attached to its boom. This line, or sheet as it is properly called, is led through a staple and then attached to the boom. Adjusters can be made from thin plastic with three fine holes drilled as shown (see earlier notes).

Set up the mizzen (aft) mast first. Pass black carpet thread through the hole in the mast and tie a reef knot on the front. Tie down these shrouds to the nails set into the hull sides. Make sure the mast is upright when viewed from ahead before tightening the knots. The thread should be pulled tight but without too much strain.

The mainmast can now be set up in the same

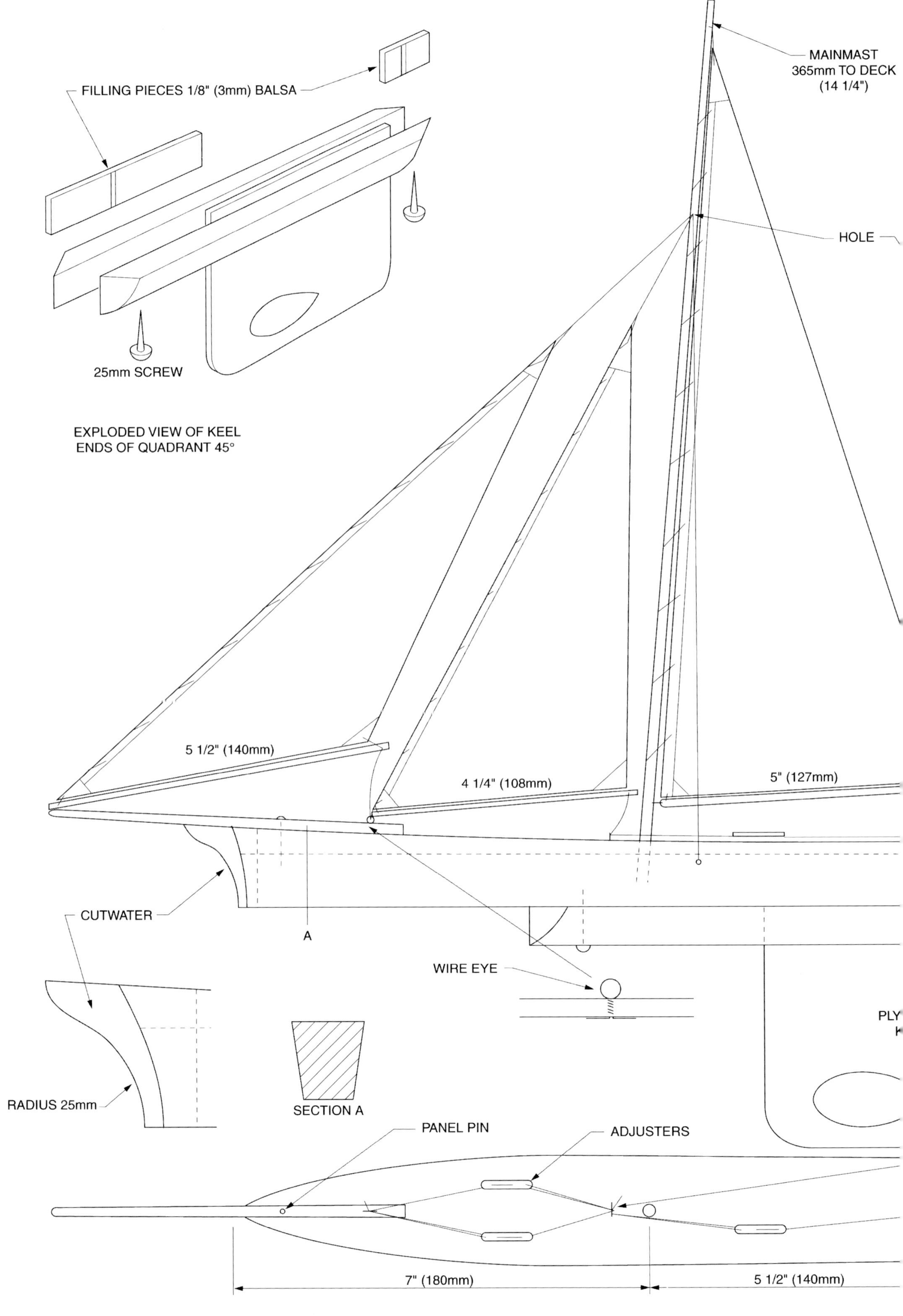

MAINMAST
365mm TO DECK
(14 1/4")
FILLING PIECES 1/8" (3mm) BALSA
HOLE
25mm SCREW
EXPLODED VIEW OF KEEL
ENDS OF QUADRANT 45°
5 1/2" (140mm)
4 1/4" (108mm)
5" (127mm)
CUTWATER
A
WIRE EYE
PLY
K
RADIUS 25mm
SECTION A
PANEL PIN
ADJUSTERS
7" (180mm)
5 1/2" (140mm)

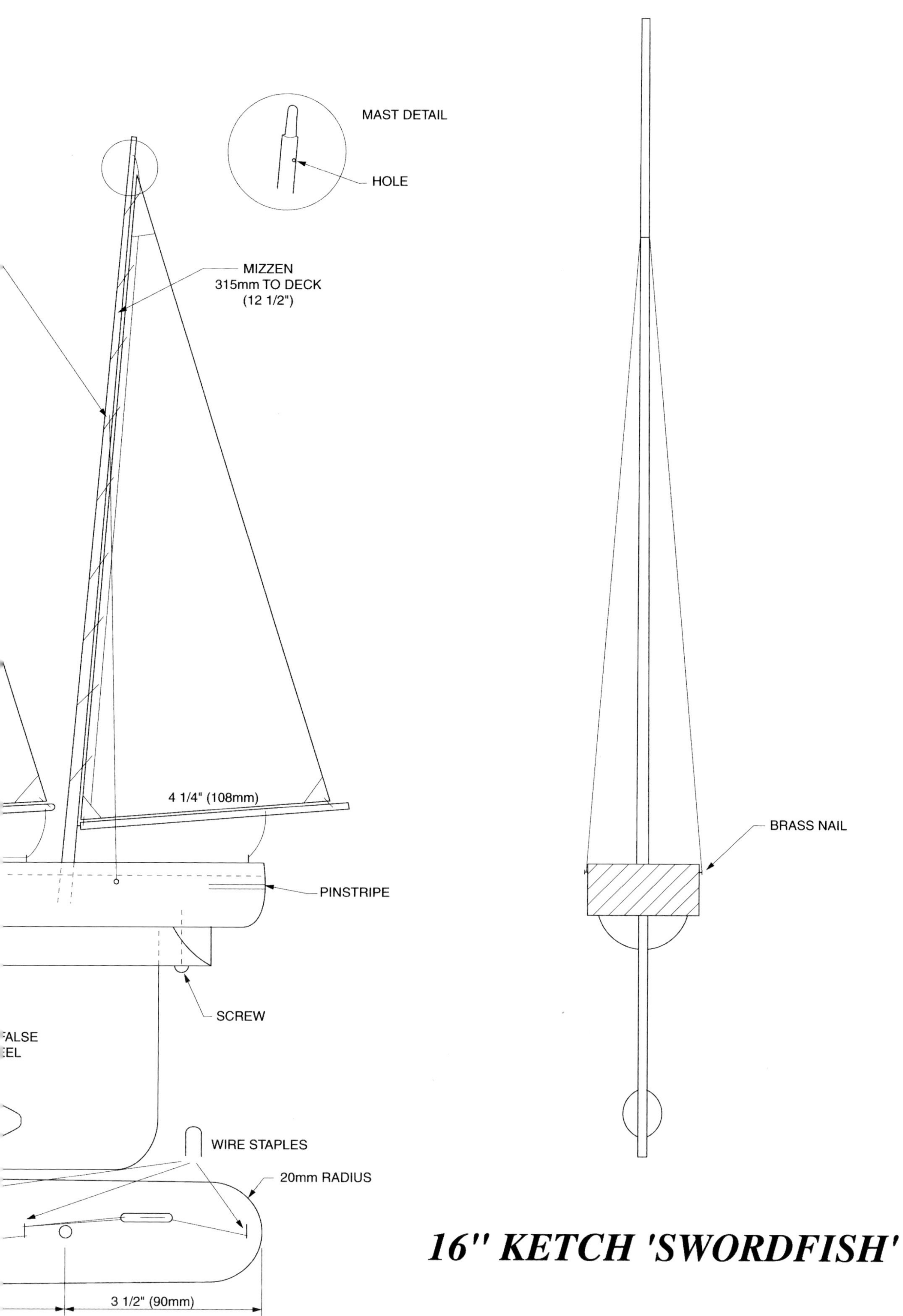

16" KETCH 'SWORDFISH'

manner. To set up the forestays pass another length of carpet thread through the hole in the mainmast and tie a reef knot in front. Pass one end through the wire ring in the bowsprit and tie off when taut. The other end is tied to the tip of the bowsprit, again nice and taut but not so tight as to pull the mainmast forward. When everything is set up correctly put a dab of glue or varnish on all the knots and allow to dry before snipping off the loose ends.

Cut cardboard patterns for the sails. If you intend to use the model for display only, greaseproof paper is best. The small size of this model often results in wet sails in rough conditions so plastic is better for the sailing version.

Use a needle to sew the bottom corner of the mizzen sail to the boom fitting where it joins the mast, using a long piece of button thread. Lace the sail to the mast using loose stitches. If they are tight the sail will not be able to swing from side to side. Tie the outer corner (clew) of the sail to the hole in the end of the boom, again, not too tight.

Complete the mizzen sail and rigging, then fit the line with a sliding adjuster so that the boom can be let out or tightened in for sailing. Take the model out into the wind to check that it all works properly and looks OK. If it does, then do the mainsail as well.

Jib sails are quite fiddly, but the drawing should give you all the information necessary. It is probably best to fix the booms to these sails before lacing them to the stays.

Sailing

Note that the keel on *Swordfish* is fixed a little more forward than it is on the mini tea clipper, This is because the clipper will only run before the wind whereas *Swordfish* has to beat across it. The keel itself is the same (see earlier text). When the ship is finished attach the keel with 1in. (25mm) No 6 roundhead screws and try her out in a reasonable breeze. Let the sails out about halfway, put her and let go. Watch carefully.

If she turns up into the wind let the mizzen sail out a bit more and try again. If she turns away from the wind tighten the mizzen in or let the jibs out a bit more. Once this tuning up has been carried out your little ship should sail a straight course.

For those who wish only to display the model the booms can be held out with fine wire to look more realistic.

Sidewinder – A 30in. Outrigger Canoe

Multi-hulls are fast, but usually a bit tricky to sail *Sidewinder* is one of the most tricky types, called the Flying Proa.

In this type, the outrigger float is always kept to windward. The theory is that its weight counterbalances the pressure on the sail. However, if the float can be kept 'flying' out of the water drag is much reduced and the boat goes faster ... a lot faster.

South Sea islanders delight in screaming along on these frail craft; with the float flying and a grinning youth clinging on to it to add weight. Unfortunately, our model does not carry any such live ballast aboard to prevent a capsize, so the sail area has been substantially reduced. Even so, she can really zip along. If the float does start to fly, she may flip over so bear this in mind if the wind is strong. In any case, this simple model makes an excellent conversation piece, in or out of water. She will provide some interesting sailing and lots of smiles.

Construction

The hull and outrigger are made from 1in. × 1in. (25mm × 25mm) planed softwood. Select timber that is clean and straight, preferably without knots. Cut to length and leave in the bath overnight to soak. Remove the next day.

While still wet place a block 30mm thick under each end of the main hull and clamp the middle down onto the bench until the centre just touches. Heavy weights can be used but you will need a lot. The float only needs blocks 25mm thick because it is shorter. After 6 to 8 hours remove timber from clamps and leave to dry for at least a day. When dry, the timber will almost have straightened out but should be left with a slight bend. Shape the ends up with a plane or surform as per the plan. It is important to leave the deck flat, with no rounded edges. The shape of the ends is not critical but try to get all four the same. Cut 3mm balsa strips to cover both hulls and glue on with PVA glue. Tape the balsa down until the glue is dry – at least 12 hours.

Use this time to cut the crossbeams from any timber about 25mm wide by 6mm thick. Drill 4mm holes as per the plan, also drill 4mm holes in the centre of plastic bottle caps. Varnish crossbeams and paint bottle caps.

Trim off surplus balsa decks on both hulls and sand all over to a smooth finish, again leave decks flat with no rounded edges. Give both hulls a coat

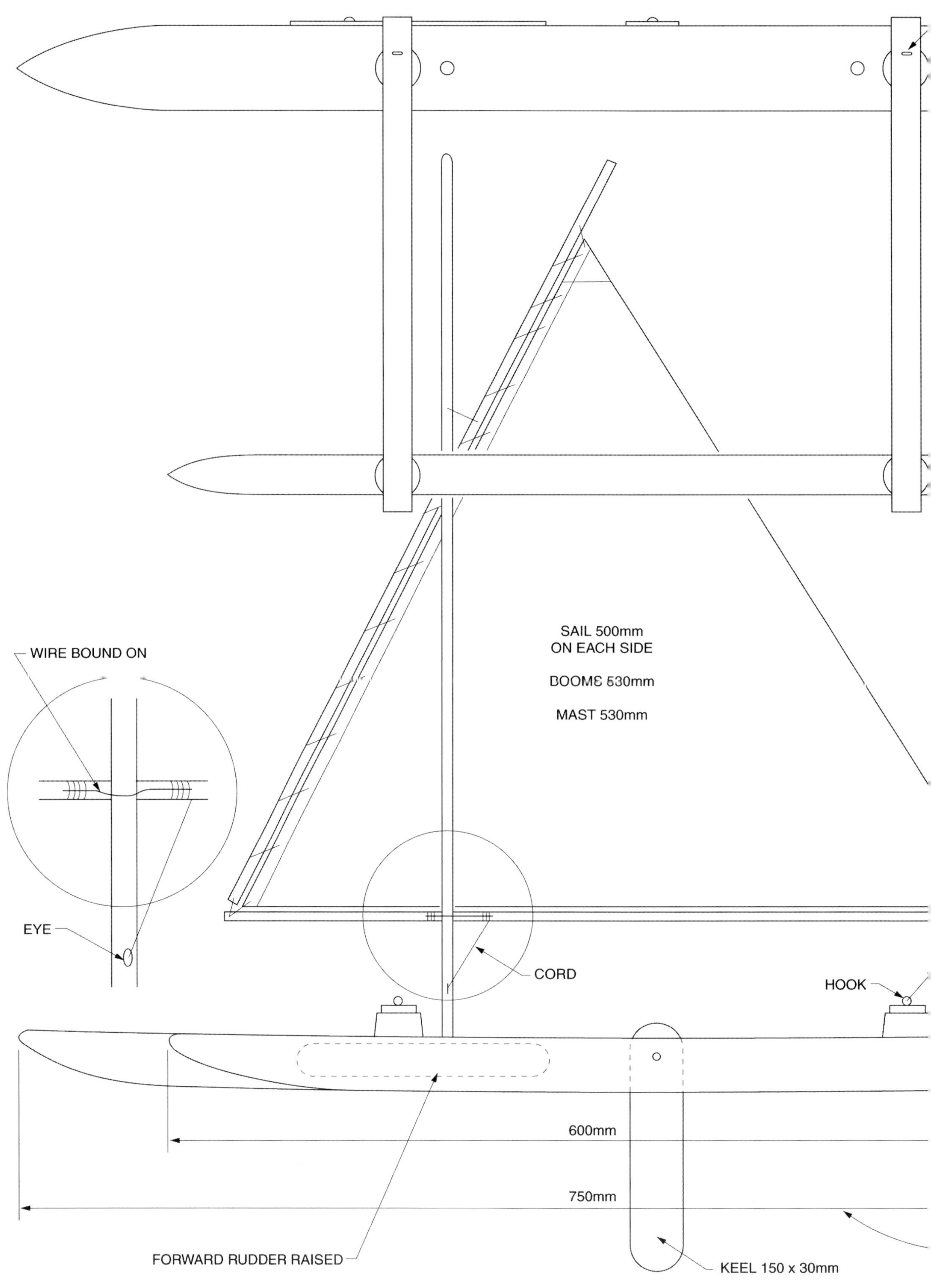

WIRE BOUND ON
SAIL 500mm
ON EACH SIDE
BOOME 530mm
MAST 530mm
EYE
CORD
HOOK
600mm
750mm
FORWARD RUDDER RAISED
KEEL 150 x 30mm

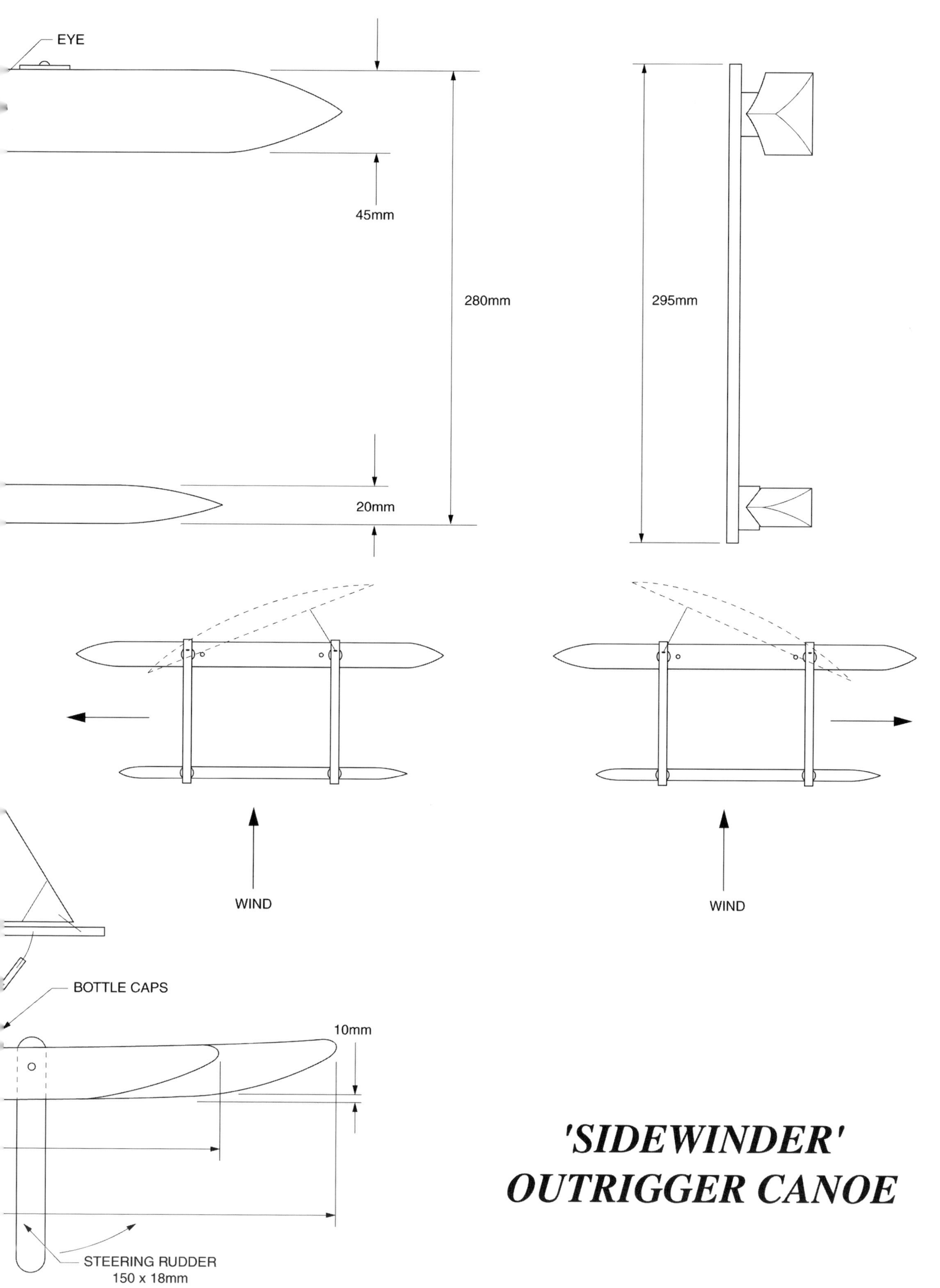

'SIDEWINDER' OUTRIGGER CANOE

of varnish or sealer, followed by undercoat and gloss paint.

Remember, this canoe is supposed to be able to travel in both directions with the outrigger float always to windward. To make this possible two mast positions are required, so you need two holes the same distance from the centre of the main hull. The mast is 8mm dowel, spars from 5mm or 6mm dowel, and the sail from any suitable cloth or plastic. The drawing should provide enough information.

Central leeboard is held by one screw and can be angled as required, and the same applies to the steering 'rudders' at each end.

Sailing

Let the sail out to 45 degrees or so, lower leeboard and rear rudder and let her go. Take a recovery line and be prepared to run. Enjoy.

The more alert among you will have noticed that the main hull on the drawing is made from 2in. × 1in. (50mm × 25inm) softwood, whereas the text only mentions 1in. × 1in. (25mm × 25mm). This is my fault entirely. In the original model, the main hull was indeed 1in. × 1in. and it went extremely well – I thought. However, in strong winds the main hull spent quite a lot of time under water. A fatter hull 2in. × 1in. was tried and although it didn't behave quite so much like a submarine, it wasn't quite so fast. The choice is yours.

No doubt, many variations are possible. For those who wish to experiment, the main hull could be made more buoyant, the crossbeams made longer, the sails bigger, additional ballast fixed to the float and so on.

An excellent article published in *Classic Boat* magazine (January 1992) featured model outriggers made by people in the Gilbert Islands. In these models, the main hull is only about 12in. (300 mm) long. There is a long bowsprit and no keel. The outrigger pole is 6 feet or 1. 8 metres long! The float is quite short.

Green coconuts are used as extra ballast lashed onto the outrigger pole to suit the strength of the wind. Enormous polythene sails send these wonderful craft skimming across a shallow turquoise lagoon at quite ridiculous speeds.

I believe they still do it. Tickets, anyone?

Spice Girl – A 24in. Trimaran

The expression 'scalded cat' could well be used to describe this boat because she certainly goes like one! Multi-hulls are usually attractive-looking craft and trimarans particularly so. They look almost like aircraft, I suppose because the cross-beams remind us of wings. *Spice Girl* is a little more complicated than the rest of the models in this book, but only because there are three hulls to make. The hulls themselves are simple boxes and very quick to build. Balsa is used almost exclusively and the whole boat is quite light, which accounts for her speed. The entire mast and sails are identical to the 'J' class sloop (see page 25). In fact, the same rig can be used for both models.

Construction

Hulls

Commence by cutting two identical main hull side panels from 3⁄32in. (2.5mm) balsa. Mark the position of all three frames on the inside faces. Cut the frames exactly to size, taking great care to get the angles the same on both sides of the centre line. Remember to draw the centre line on each frame. Tape the ends of the side panels together. Push the centre frame into place and hold with pins, then pin the other two frames into place. When all is fairly well lined up, remove one frame at a time, cement and replace. Run plenty of cement into the ends, place extra pins and tape to hold everything in place until the cement is completely dry.

Next, cut two panels for the bottom, each 1¼in. (32mm) wide. Pin one panel along the bottom with the machine-cut edge in line with all the frame centre lines and the ends. This should pull the hull into perfect alignment. Pin on the other panel with the machine-cut edge also on the centre line. Look inside the hull. If all seems to be lined up properly mark the position of all the frames on the inside of the bottom panels.

Mark out the slot for the centre-board also. Run a ballpoint pen round the hull onto the bottom panels. Remove the panels one at a time and cut away the waste, leaving 1mm for final trimming. Cement the panels back exactly as they were, then sand the edges flush with the sides when dry. Take great care not to damage the side panels at this stage.

Make the mast tube from an old felt-tip pen or ballpoint pen. This should accept ¼in. (6mm)

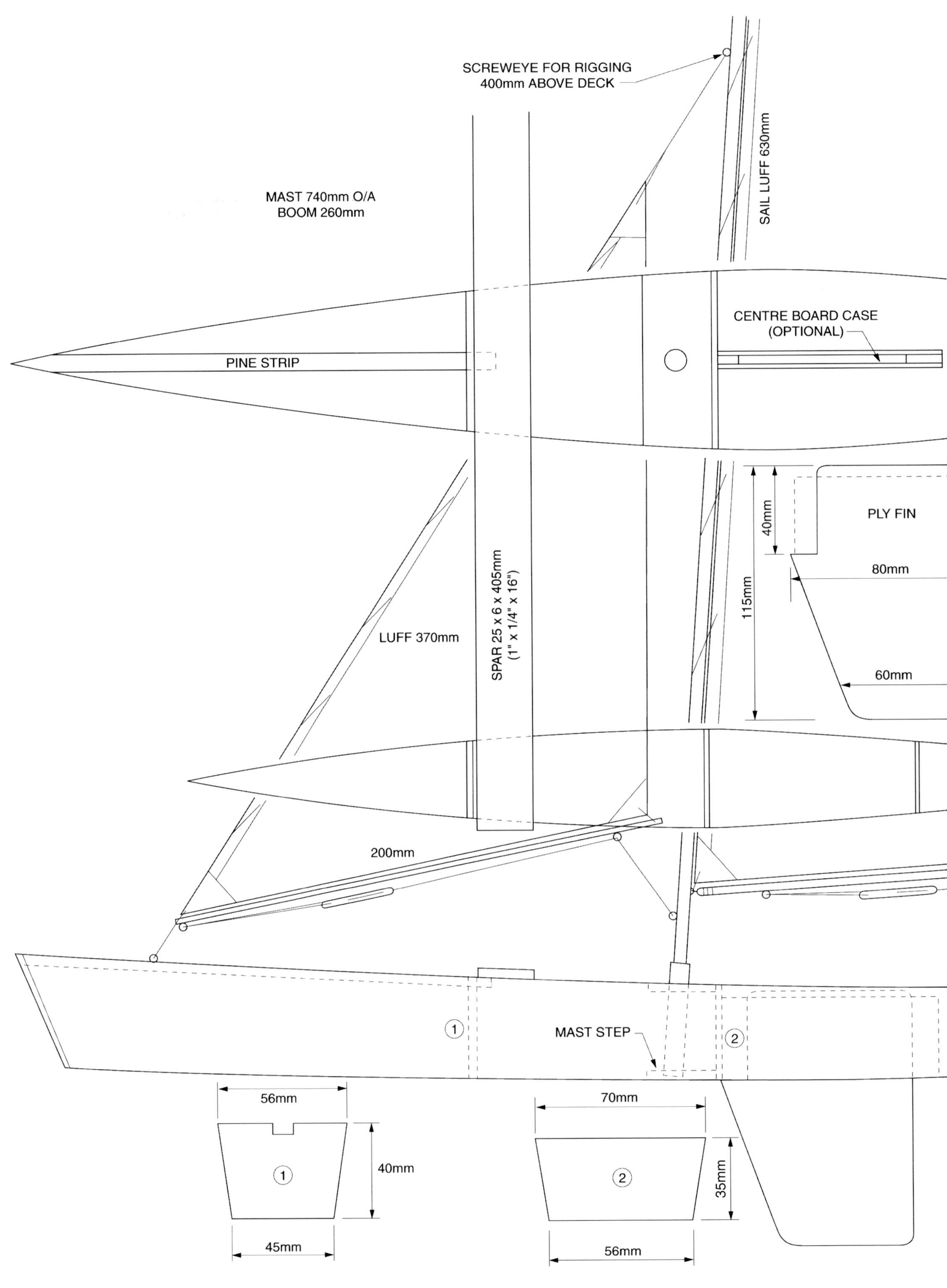

SCREWEYE FOR RIGGING
400mm ABOVE DECK
SAIL LUFF 630mm
MAST 740mm O/A
BOOM 260mm
CENTRE BOARD CASE
(OPTIONAL)
PINE STRIP
PLY FIN
40mm
80mm
115mm
LUFF 370mm
SPAR 25 x 6 x 405mm
(1" x 1/4" x 16")
60mm
200mm
1
MAST STEP
2
56mm
70mm
40mm
35mm
45mm
56mm

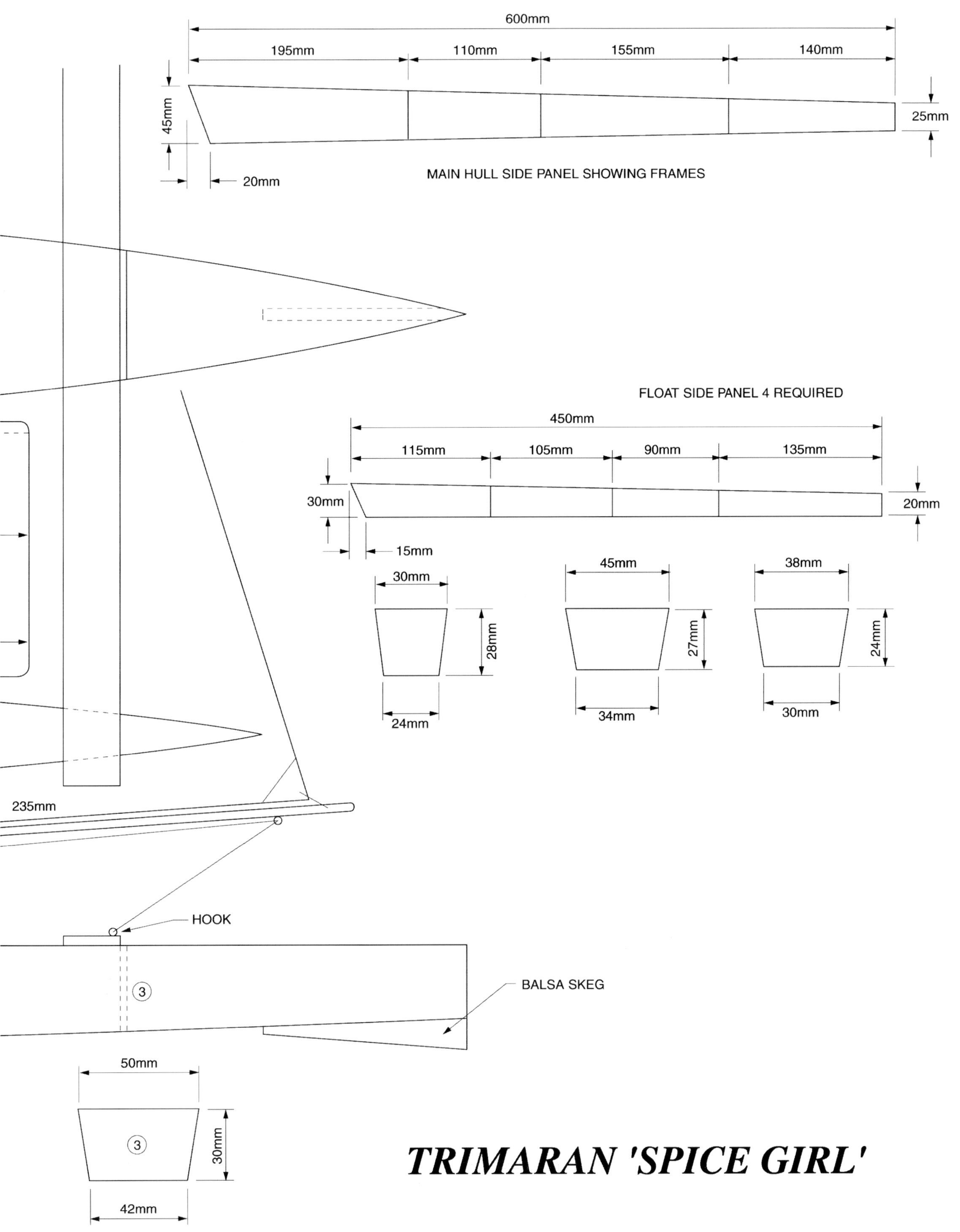

TRIMARAN 'SPICE GIRL'

dowel. Set the tube up in a drilled balsa block cemented to the hull floor. Fit another balsa beam across the top of the hull with a hole drilled for the tube. Place the mast in the tube while setting up so that the correct angle of rake (backward slant) can be given before the cement sets. *Araldite* makes a stronger bond for this joint. Remember, the mast should be upright when viewed from ahead.

The prototype has a centre-board case so that the plywood centre-board can be removed, but this is optional. The hull was also left open between frames 2 and 3 so that additional ballast or a 'crew' could be carried, but again, the hull can be completely decked over and the keel remain fixed, if you prefer.

Speaking of ballast, a balsa hull is so light I thought it prudent to add a little weight. A piece of 1in. × 1in. (22mm × 22mm) planed softwood 3in. (75mm) long was glued on the hull floor in front of mast step and another similar piece glued in the rear compartment.

Float hulls are made in exactly the same way (but no ballast) except that the bottom panel is in one piece. A central line is drawn in ballpoint pen along the panel to assist in getting the shape true.

All the hulls should get a coat of clear polyurethane varnish and an undercoat inside before the decks are fitted. When the decks are on, the crossbeam spars should be glued straight down onto the balsa deck before varnishing. Pine or hardwood can be used for these.

Great care and measurement must be taken when fitting the spars. Glue them onto the main hull first exactly square with the centre line. They must be parallel to each other and level when viewed from ahead. This is most important.

When the spars are firmly fixed on the floats can be added. Check that the bow and stern of each float is the same distance from the centre line of the main hull. Cement one float on first with a support under it to hold it up beneath the spars. When dry fit the other one in exactly the same way. Everything can now be varnished over, three coats plus undercoat, plus gloss.

Mast and rigging

Mast and rigging are quite straightforward as described earlier and should present no problems.

Sails

Greaseproof paper can be used on this model as it is unlikely to turn over and soak the sails.

Sailing

Sailing trials were recently carried out on a big lake (my local sailing club) and in a fresh breeze. Several members came out to watch and were suitably impressed. She is certainly fast and I had to do a lot of brisk walking across mud – much to their amusement, of course!

An 18in. Scow

I have always been fascinated by the unusual or unconventional. Show me a car with only one wheel at the back, an aeroplane that looks as though it flies backwards or a traction engine painted bright yellow and I will be riveted. Even the quirky French 2CV car still gives me a lift when I spot one. It therefore follows that boats that aren't pointed at the ends have received my close attention.

Skimming dishes, or scows as such vessels are called, are quite simple to make and can go like smoke in the right conditions. From a scow's point of view, the right conditions are smooth water and sailing almost upright.

This model really should have two different sets of sails – one large set for light winds and a small set for stronger conditions, because she doesn't like sailing on one ear. It is quite easy to make two complete rigs and use the one most suitable on the day.

Construction

Cut the two identical sides from ⅛in. (3mm) balsa, all the frames will be the same length as the sides are completely straight. Fix frames 1 and 4 with pins. Make sure the hull is not twisted before these are cemented in place. This is important because once a twist appears it is not easy to correct. Keep checking for twist. The secret is not to force anything and make sure all the frames are dead square at the ends.

Cut the two long floor panels, each 2½in. (65mm) wide. Remove the thin pieces from each panel to accept the keel. Cement these panels in place. Next, cut and fix frames 2, 3 and 4.

Fix the rear floor panel with the grain running across the boat. All floor and deck panels are from 2.5mm balsa. The curved bottom panel forward of frame 1 is also laid across the boat. Because of the curvature, the panels should be cut into 20mm wide strips and sanded smooth when the cement is dry.

Fix the transom and reinforcing strips across the bow. Make the mast tube from an old ballpoint or felt-tip pen. Set this up in a drilled block glued to the floor and another wide drilled strip across the boat at deck level. Put the mast in the tube to assist in getting it vertical when viewed from ahead and raked backwards when viewed from the side.

Make the keel from ⅛in. (3mm) balsa and let in the 4oz lead weight. Note the 8mm strip across the

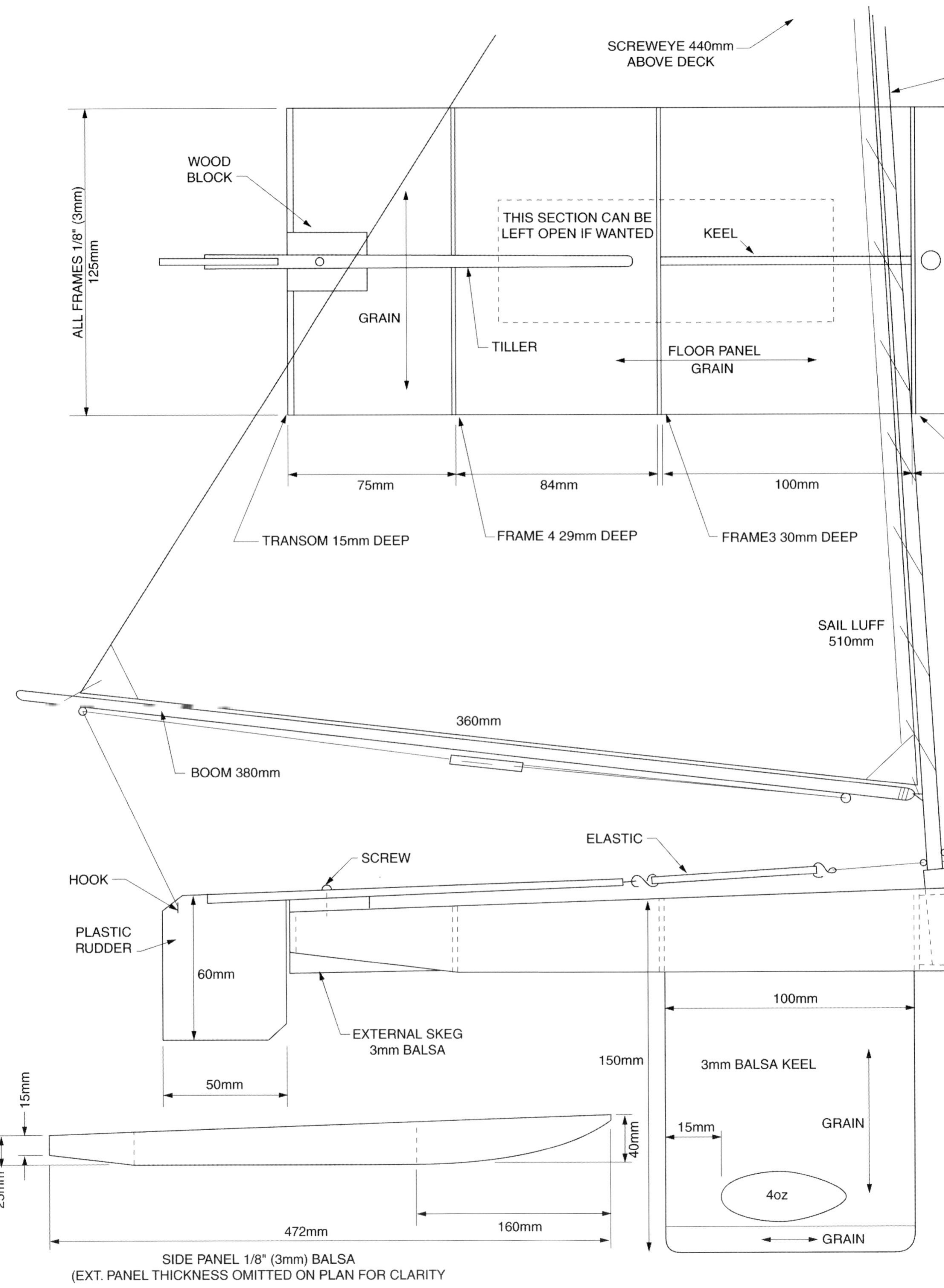
SCREWEYE 440mm
ABOVE DECK
WOOD
BLOCK
ALL FRAMES 1/8" (3mm)
125mm
THIS SECTION CAN BE
LEFT OPEN IF WANTED
KEEL
GRAIN
TILLER
FLOOR PANEL
GRAIN
75mm
84mm
100mm
TRANSOM 15mm DEEP
FRAME 4 29mm DEEP
FRAME3 30mm DEEP
SAIL LUFF
510mm
360mm
BOOM 380mm
ELASTIC
SCREW
HOOK
PLASTIC
RUDDER
60mm
EXTERNAL SKEG
3mm BALSA
100mm
150mm
3mm BALSA KEEL
50mm
GRAIN
15mm
15mm
40mm
25mm
4oz
GRAIN
472mm
160mm
SIDE PANEL 1/8" (3mm) BALSA
(EXT. PANEL THICKNESS OMITTED ON PLAN FOR CLARITY

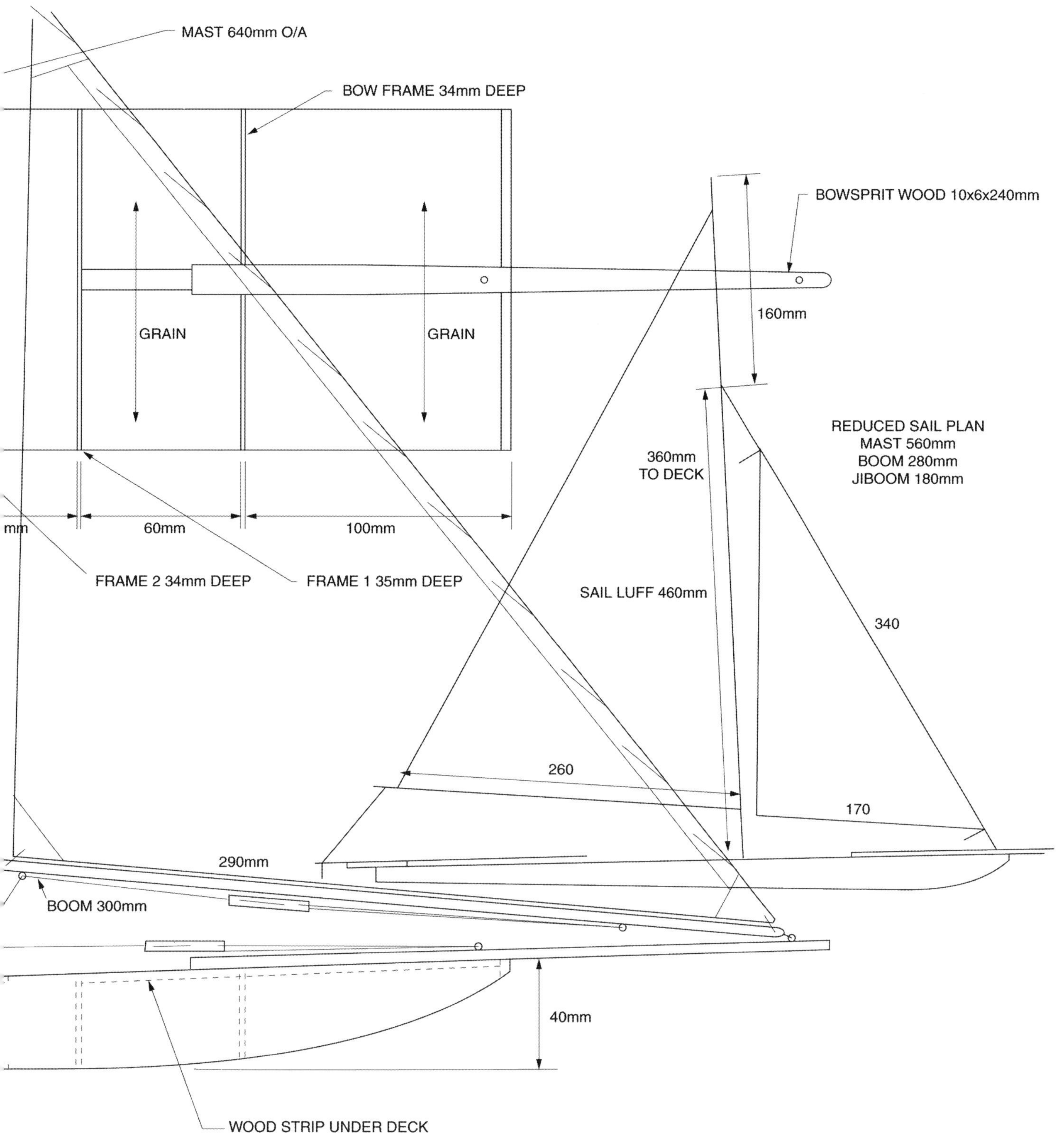

LIGHT WEATHER SAILS SHOWN

SCOW 'WINKLE PICKER'

bottom of the keel to help stop it warping. Fit the keel in place firmly (and upright) and fit reinforcement strips along the top.

Fit the pine strip in the bow to accept screweyes for rigging or bowsprit. Varnish the boat inside and out twice, then undercoat.

Cut and fit the deck panels 3⁄32in. (2.5mm) balsa. I left the centre sections open, but this is optional. You may wish to deck completely over. It isn't a bad idea to wedge polystyrene blocks into the closed sections to stiffen the hull and make it unsinkable. This is entirely up to you and not strictly necessary.

Sand the deck and edges smooth and varnish at least three coats. Fix the wood block to the stern to carry the rudder assembly, also glue on the bowsprit. Complete painting and varnishing.

The rudder assembly is the simplest possible and will provide a good measure of self-steering. Tension to keep it straight is provided by an elastic band and the tension is adjusted as required by a slider on the cord.

The theory is, the boom of the sail pulls the rudder over just enough to stop the boat turning into the wind. It needs to be tuned up during sailing trials and works quite well.

Sails and rigging follow the basic format already described. The choice of plastic or greaseproof paper sails is up to you. The sail plan is quite large, but kept fairly low aspect.

Sailing

The performance of this boat is surprisingly good and will provide some exciting sailing.

Despite the conventional opinion that scows aren't supposed to like sailing 'on one ear, this model seems to positively enjoy it.

Nautilus – An 8in. Galleon

Any serious scale modellers should kindly leave the room now.

Nautilus is a little charmer, but doesn't pretend to be authentic. She can be built by anyone although children will need some help – and would probably prefer to call her a pirate ship.

Once the hull has been cut from 3in. × 1in. (75mm × 25mm) softwood, the hardest part of the work is over. A decision has to be made now as to whether this model is going to be sailed or not. For the display-only model, the choice of materials can include card and paper to a much greater degree but those wishing to go a-voyaging need to use more durable materials. The small size of this model means the deck will be frequently awash when afloat and cardboard parts will soon look battered.

Construction

Care should be taken to proceed in the following order.

1 Cut hull from 3in. × 1in. (75mm × 25mm) planed softwood 8in. (200mm) long. The ends will probably need to be cut by an adult. Rounding off the 'corners' on the bow is optional.

2 Drill holes for masts to suit the diameter of dowel (4mm or 5mm). Note the mizzen mast should lean backwards towards the stern.

3 Cut masts and spars to length. Taper top part of masts and both ends of spars. Lay masts and yards flat to assemble. Glue yards using a generous blob of glue and leave to dry (really dry – several hours at least).

4. Drill hole in plastic (lemonade) bottle cap for mainmast's crow's nest. This should be a reasonably tight fit on the mast. Paint the inside of the cap a light colour and decorate the outside in two colours as per the drawing. Do not fix yet.

   Note: if shrouds are to be fitted, leave the crow's nest off until they are tied on.

5 Cut transom from balsa or plywood (card can be used for the non-sailing version). Glue on.

6 Cut stern castle side pieces, using balsa or strong card. Stick on wales (strips) and other decoration before attaching the castle sides to the ship. The castle sides should be painted both sides with undercoat, gloss or emulsion paint. Do not fix yet.

7 Stick on bowsprit (lolly stick) and bow pieces (matchsticks or strips cut from lolly stick).

8 Fix masts in and check if upright when viewed from ahead. Note the angle across the ship of the mizzen mast yard.

9 Varnish all over twice. Paint hull sides and transom keeping paint off the deck.

10 Fit rigging if selected. Tap in two gimp pins (small flathead nails) in the ship's side as shown. Using carpet thread, tie one end to the

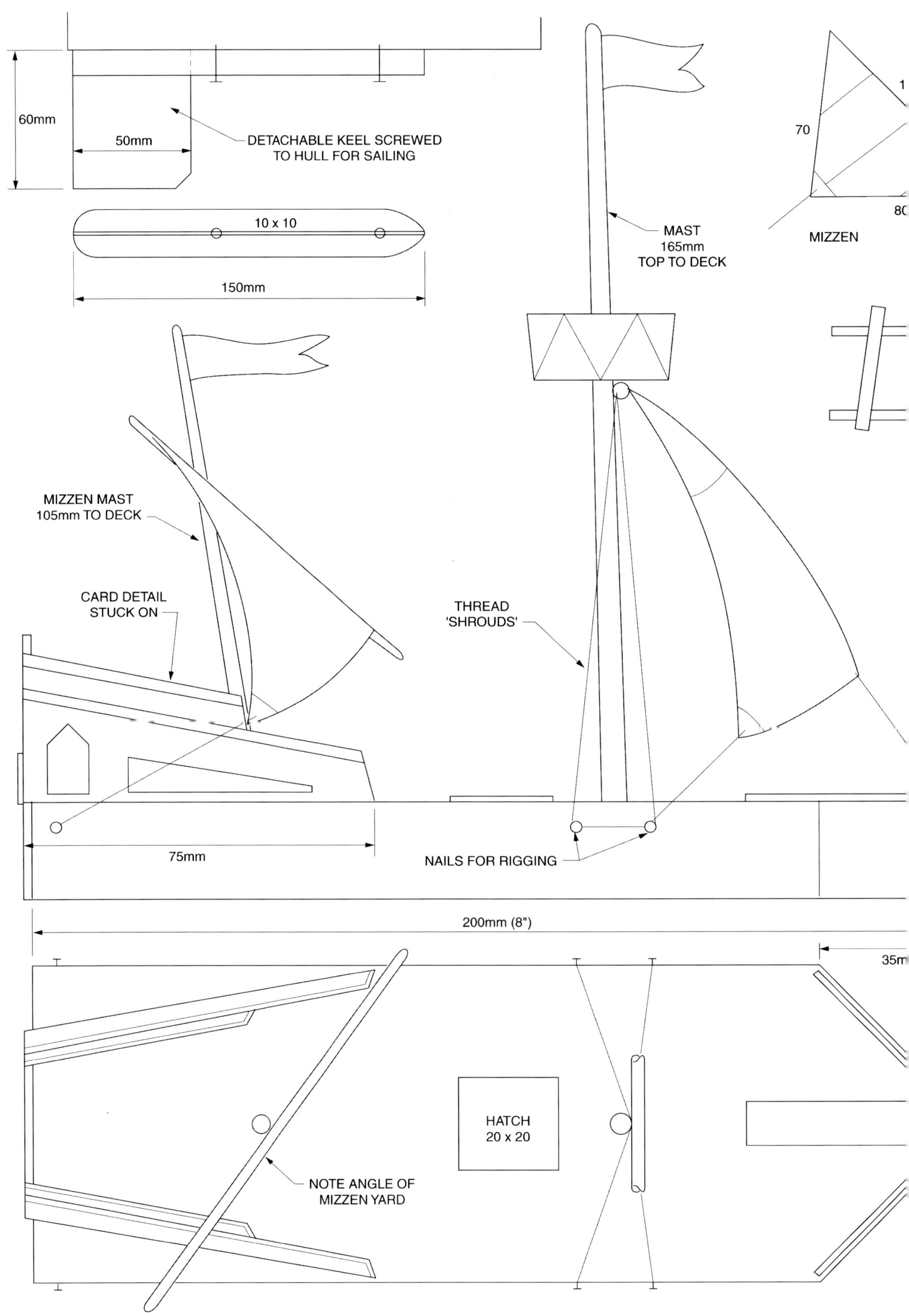
60mm
50mm
DETACHABLE KEEL SCREWED
TO HULL FOR SAILING
10 x 10
150mm
MAST
165mm
TOP TO DECK
70
MIZZEN
MIZZEN MAST
105mm TO DECK
CARD DETAIL
STUCK ON
THREAD
'SHROUDS'
75mm
NAILS FOR RIGGING
200mm (8")
HATCH
20 x 20
NOTE ANGLE OF
MIZZEN YARD

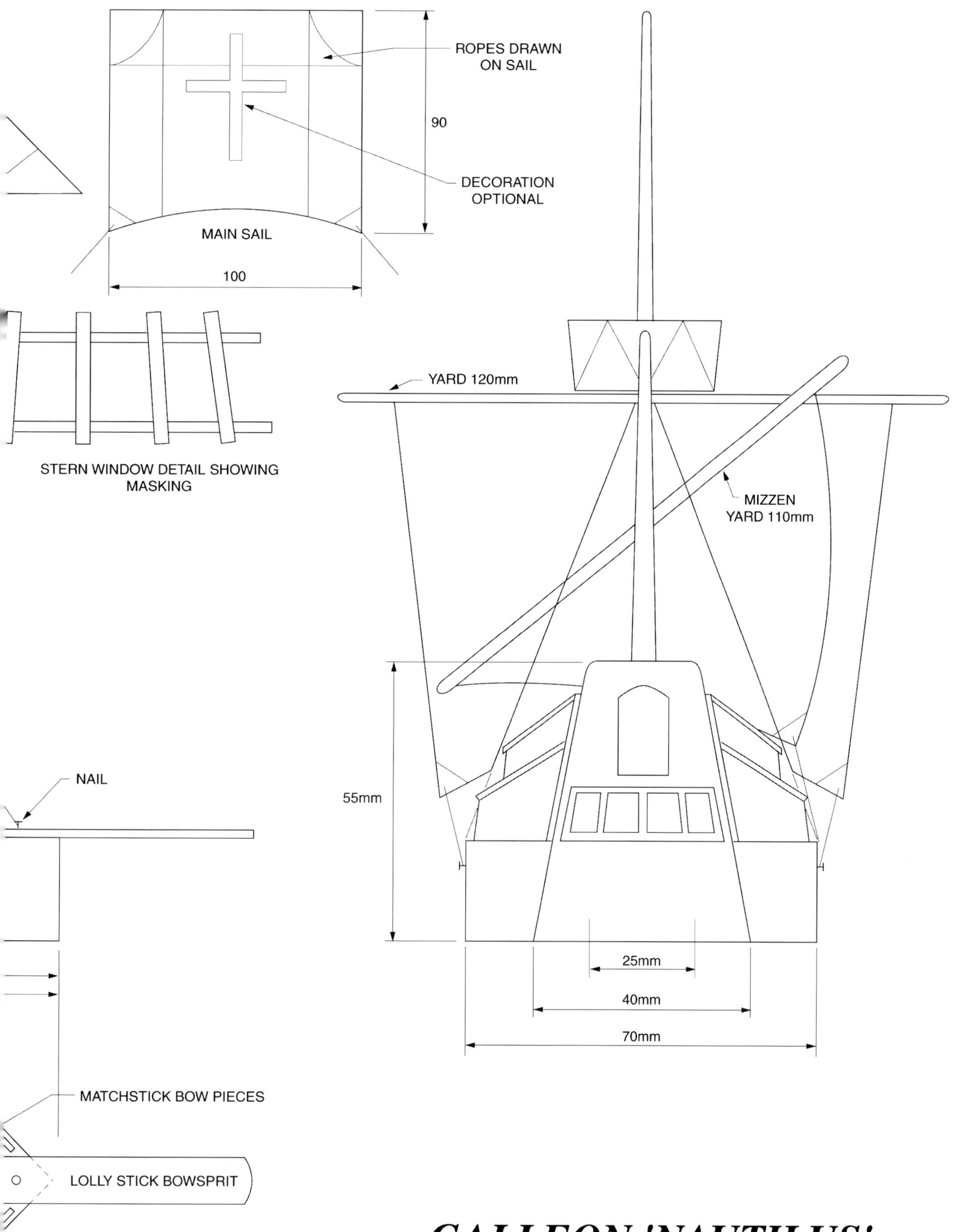

GALLEON 'NAUTILUS'

nail in the bows. Take the thread over the mainyard from behind, round the front of the mast and then down to the forward nail on the ship's side. Take one turn round this and back to the rear nail. The thread now goes up to the mainyard again and down to the forward nail on the other side. Back to the other nail and finally up to the mainyard. Tie off above the yard, glue and snip off the loose end.

The crow's nest can now be slid down the mast to rest on top of the yard. Glue with PVA.

I hope you followed all that – simple really.

11 Stern castle sides should now be completed and glued on using PVA.

12 The windows across the stern are a most attractive addition. Mark out carefully on strong white card as per the drawing. Do not cut out yet. Stick a short length of insulating tape onto a smooth surface and slice into narrow strips (2mm). Stick these across and round the shape as shown. Lightly spray over with blue car spray or stipple with an almost dry brush. Remove strips. Two edges of each window should be highlighted with black ballpoint pen.

Cut out the completed stern gallery window and stick it onto the transom. Looks fabulous, doesn't it?

13 Cut and fix the hatch in the deck – thick card will do. Paint green or brown.

14 Varnish the hull and stern castle all over to further waterproof it.

15 Cut sails from greaseproof paper. Reinforce bottom corners with masking tape and attach button thread 'ropes' by either sticking them under the masking tape or tying. Decoration on sails can be painted on or sticky tape can be used. Glue the sails along the top of the yard with PVA glue. When dry tie the ropes (proper term 'sheets') to nails as shown.

16 Make and glue on a couple of coloured flags (flying forward, please) from paper, crinkled up for better effect.

17 Make the keel if the sailing version has been selected. Paint a dark colour and fix to the hull with small screws. The keel should be made and fitted at an early stage in construction, removed and laid aside until the model is completed.

Note: Sailing without the keel fitted is not advisable. She will probably turn sideways on to the wind and could capsize.

Sailing

We can't expect a Grand Prix performance from such a tiny ship but she will forge along gallantly in a decent wind. No doubt, many variations are possible. A racing version would probably need more and bigger sails. Anyway, do your own thing and enjoy it – that's what it's all about.

Appendix

Metric/imperial measurement conversion table for the 'J' class sloop

For the benefit of those who prefer to use imperial measurement a list of all equivalents appearing on the drawings for the 'J' class sloop is found below.

12mm	½in.	130mm	5 ⅛in.
25mm	1in.	160mm	6 5/16in.
26mm	1 1/32in.	165mm	6¼in.
28mm	1⅛in.	180mm	7⅛in.
30mm	1 3/16in.	200mm	8in.
35mm	1⅜in.	210mm	8 5/16in.
40mm	1 9/16in.	230mm	9 1/16in.
45mm	1¾in.	235mm	9¼in.
50mm	2in.	270mm	10⅝in.
55mm	2 3/16in.	370mm	14⅝in.
65mm	2 9/16in.	400mm	15¾in.
85mm	3⅜in.	600mm	23¾in.
95mm	3¾in.	630mm	25in.
120mm	4¾in.	740mm	29¼in.

Is metric better? Call me François!

Other titles of interest from Nexus Special Interests

Model Ships from Scratch Scott Robertson

In this first title, Scott Robertson shows you how you can build an end product of fascination, history, skill and value using low-cost materials and a minimum of tools from scratch. The text is packed with useful hints and tips which, together with a number of detailed drawings and photographs, provides a very practical guide to the art and craft of model ship building.

1994, ISBN 1-85486-105-0, 160 pages + 4pp colour plates, A4 paperback

Historic Model Ships from Scratch Scott Robertson NEW!

In this, Scott Robertson's second book on the subject of making model ships from scratch, you are given a wide variety of interesting facts and instructions including the old pastime of putting a model ship into a bottle. Together with the detailed drawings and photographs of many model ships made by the author, plus close-ups of deck details and fittings, this book will appeal to both beginners and amateur modelmakers.

1998, ISBN 1-85486-187-5, 144 pages + 4pp colour plates, A4 paperback

The Period Ship Handbook Keith Julier

Have you ever been put off by the thought of all that planking and rigging? This book helps the beginner and the more experienced alike to overcome some of the real, and the mythical, problems of model ship construction. Using a number of commercially available kits as a basis for discussion, the book provides detailed, step-by-step procedures for making each model. Invaluable for beginners and all modelmakers with an interest in building period ship models without the need for sophisticated workshop facilities.

1992, ISBN 1-85486-081-X, 208 pages + 4pp colour plates, A4 paperback

The Period Ship Handbook 2 Keith Julier

A further venture into the world of static model sailing ships, offering guidance to the beginner and discussion on modelmaking for the more experienced. Suggestions on expanding the tool kit from the basic essentials towards more sophisticated equipment are followed by an overall view of commercially available kits and their selection. The main body of the book is devoted to the building of ten models, all available in kit form. Each vessel selected has something different to offer the modelmaker, whether it be ornamentation or miniature authentic carpentry. Information is provided on the English Rate system and the book concludes with a summary of more modelling techniques.

1995, ISBN 1-85486-132-8, 144 pages + 4pp colour plates, A4 paperback

*The titles listed above should be available from all good bookshops.
In the event of difficulty, please contact Nexus Special Interests, Books Division,
Nexus House, Azalea Drive, Swanley, Kent BR8 8HU. Tel: 01322 660070.*